CHINA TO-DAY

THROUGH CHINESE EYES

BY

Dr. T. T. LEW   Prof. Y. Y. TSU
Prof. HU SHIH   Dr. CHENG CHING YI

LONDON :

STUDENT CHRISTIAN MOVEMENT

32, RUSSELL SQUARE, W.C.1

1922

First published November, 1922
Second Impression, March, 1923

PRINTED IN GREAT BRITAIN BY
HEADLEY BROTHERS, 18, DEVONSHIRE STREET, E.C.
AND ASHFORD, KENT.

CONTENTS

CHAPTER   PAGE

     FOREWORD   -   -   -   -   -   -   -   7

     WHO'S WHO   -   -   -   -   -   -   -   9

I   CHINA TO-DAY. Reprinted from *The Life Journal*   -   -   -   -   -   -   11

II   CHINA'S RENAISSANCE. T. T. Lew   -   21

III   THE LITERARY REVOLUTION IN CHINA. Hu Shih   -   -   -   -   -   -   54

IV   THE CONFUCIAN GOD-IDEA. Y. Y. Tsu   67

V   PRESENT TENDENCIES IN CHINESE BUDDHISM. Y. Y. Tsu   -   -   -   86

VI   THE IMPRESSION OF CHRISTIANITY MADE UPON THE CHINESE PEOPLE THROUGH CONTACT WITH THE CHRISTIAN NATIONS OF THE WEST. Reprinted from *The Life Journal*   -   -   111

VII   THE CHINESE CHURCH. Cheng Ching Yi   122

FOREWORD

For the delegates of the World's Student Christian Federation Conference in Peking, in April of this year, the Chinese Student Christian Movement prepared some account of the "New Tide of Thought," the great Renaissance Movement which is sweeping through China to-day, and of the economic, intellectual and religious forces which form the background of it.

By their permission we reprint striking articles contributed by four of the leaders of the younger generation of present-day China, and two articles from *The Life Journal*, the organ of a group of Christian leaders of the Renaissance Movement in Peking.

Those who would understand the intellectual, religious and economic forces which are moulding Chinese life and thought at this time cannot do better than study this Chinese account of them. The following is a short account of the writers.

WHO'S WHO

Dr. T. T. Lew is Dean of the Theological Faculty in Peking University ; Professor in another College ; Pastor of a Church, and Editor of *The Life*—a paper which is known throughout China, and is the organ of the Christian leaders of the Renaissance. Dr. Lew is recognised as one of the ablest and most prophetic members in the Chinese Church.

Professor Hu Shih (Suh Hu). One of the ablest and most devoted of the Renaissance leaders. He is not a Christian, but has many Christian friends and much of the spirit of Christ. He has done more than any other single individual to replace the old classical style in literature by the *Bai Hwa* or "plain language." In 1916 he took the revolutionary step of publishing a poem in the vernacular and thus showing how it was the best expression of living thought. He has suffered persecution for his boldness in disregarding any conventions which hinder progress. The spread of the Renaissance Movement to all classes is largely due to his courageous efforts, which have put the new thought not into the language of the pedant and scholar, but of the common man ; a change as significant and as potent for good as the change from Latin to English in our own country at the beginning of the European Renaissance.

PROFESSOR Y. Y. TSU. An old scholar of Union Seminary, New York, is a professor at St. John's College, Shanghai—the foster-mother of so many of China's ablest young leaders. He is one of the first Chinese theologians—and his clear thinking and thorough knowledge and understanding of Confucianism and Buddhism are laying sound foundations for the theology of the Chinese Church.

DR. CHENG CHING YI. One of the greatest figures in the Chinese Church. He is recognised as a leader whom all sections trust and delight to follow. He was a representative of China at the Edinburgh Conference in 1910, and Chairman of the recent National Conference of Christian workers in Shanghai. He knows more about and is probably more representative of the Chinese Church than any other Christian leader in China.

I

CHINA TO-DAY

It is a significant fact which deserves our most serious attention that the Federation Conference should be held at this time in China. China of to-day in more than one aspect deserves the study of the members of the Federation who have the interest of the world at heart.

Politically, China is in a state of difficulty. To a casual observer the difficulty consists of disunity, inefficiency and weakness. One hears about the two governments, one in Peking known as the Central Government, and one in Canton known as the Southern Government. One also hears of the undue power of the military governors and the super-tuchuns who hold sway in the various parts of the country. They even meddle with the authority of the Central Government. There is lack of unity in policy and in ideals.

One also sees and hears about the inefficiency which is apparent everywhere from the Central Government down to the local administration of a city. You will find antiquated methods being still used alongside of modern methods. Obstacles and interruptions are abundant, hindering the successful through all the troubles and experiences of the effort. China also has world democracy as her ultimate hope, and in that hope she finds encouragement and stimulus in her efforts to reorganise and develop herself.

Intellectually, one can also find things open to criticism. The illiteracy of the masses is still very high. The educational opportunities for the mass are far from satisfactory and sufficient. Dense ignorance is prevalent. Educational equipment and support of institutions of all grades are not only insufficient but even uncertain in some places. Superstitions due to lack of knowledge are still rampant, affecting individual and social living. Poverty due to lack of scientific economics and technical knowledge, together with other causes, is all prevailing. The general view of a candid observer is discouraging.

But when we look deeper into the situation we immediately feel the beating of a strong pulse. China as a nation in fact, is in an age of a great renaissance. The time-honoured custom and firmly established habit of respecting learning and the learned has not in any way diminished. The desire for knowledge and the diligence to acquire it is increasing in intensity. During the last five years great change has been brought about in connection with the life of the Chinese people. Instead of merely seeking after a knowledge of external things, the Renaissance Movement has been changing the people's general attitude toward life. This is the culmination of a long process of intellectual revolution which has been going on ever since China came into contact with the West. The emphasis has passed from the desire merely for the products of science, to the appreciation of the principles of science, from the thirst after the achievements of western civilisation to the attempts to interpret the meaning and value of such achievements. The Movement now is to pierce into the deeper meaning of modern science and philosophy, not merely to adopt its superficial externals. Along with this, there has been also a marked change of attitude toward the material and spiritual achievements of the Chinese race. This change is still going on. It is merely a beginning. The Movement has put up as its platform four big tasks, namely, the reorganisation, the re-statement and the re-evaluation of Chinese civilisation ; the importation of western civilisation with critical examination of it; a thorough and scientific study of theories and facts ; a reconstruction of individual and social life. This is an ambitious platform but the progress thus far has been encouraging.

Educational work has been greatly advanced. In spite of the lack of funds, schools multiply. The last two or three years have witnessed the birth of several institutions of higher learning. Newspapers have increased both in number and in circulation.

The Bai Hwa* Movement has not only put knowledge at the disposal of the masses by giving them a more effective tool, and a tool easier to acquire, but has also changed the attitude of the people toward knowledge. Knowledge has been made a democratic property belonging to all. No less than two hundred periodicals have come into existence in the last four years as the response to this Movement, covering all the subjects which anybody in China cares to discuss—from the scientific treatment of an historical incident centuries ago to the latest economic or political theory known to the world. Foreign books are translated in large numbers. Not only are these books better translated than ever before, but a wiser selection is being made. In scholarship we have witnessed the production of some very valuable contributions to the re-interpretation of Chinese philosophy and Chinese history. A beginning is also made on the methodology of studying things Chinese and things Western. Leaders in education have made a distinct advance in conducting thorough surveys of educational conditions and needs. They are hard at work at genuine constructive measures and are making fundamental changes in educational policy. The National Educational Association has also passed a measure which involves a radical reform of the whole educational system. The emphasis upon vocational

* "plain language," see pp. 9, 27, 63.

education represented by the China Vocational Education Association, is also gaining headway in various parts of China. In short, China has in the last few years attained a clearer vision of the goal of intellectual development, has received a new driving force to push on to this goal, and has acquired an unprecedented freedom with which to reach this goal.

Religiously, one can even state in stronger terms the darker side. The historical religions in China have shown an impotency and lack of vitality. Superstitious beliefs still hold power over the ignorant masses, not for better living but as a bondage and an obstacle to the free development of the individual. Old standards of morality have received shocks from the invasions of modern ideas. Everywhere one sees discrepancies and maladjustments. The craving after material property has outrun the desire for spiritual enlightenment. Destructive forces have come in from various directions without the sign of constructive relief measures. Indifference to religion and the contempt for religion is gradually spreading on the one hand, and a strange outcropping of superstitious sects preying upon the ignorant masses is found on the other hand. It is indeed a situation in which religion may be said to be at a low ebb.

Yet, the brighter side has never been brighter. Many superstitions have been destroyed by the flooding in of intellectual light. Political and social change have also shattered idols of centuries' standing. Thoughtful people are coming more and more to see the need of moral strength for the task of reconstruction. It is a significant fact that the older religions have started reform within themselves. Reinterpretation and reorganisation have become the battle-cry of the followers of these religions. No less than half a dozen new journals have come into existence within the last few years in Buddhism alone. While materialistic philosophy and anti-theistic teaching are gaining headway, there are increasing numbers of young men and women who turn their faces toward religion for the solution of life's problem. School girls and educated men in the prime of life have left their schools and their occupations and joined the ascetic life of Buddhism. The attempt to reorganise Confucianism into a religious church, although it has met with much opposition, is yet gaining adherents in many quarters. All these point toward an increasing sense of religious need felt by the people at large. In addition to that there is also the recognition of the universal element in religion. An organisation has been born with the aim of unifying the old religions and calls itself the " Society for the Common Good." While the organisation has not yet achieved any result worth serious consideration, yet it is at least a sign of the desire for religious unity. While the

Renaissance Movement in the main pays very little respect to religion, and does not recognise the necessity of religion, yet by its very principle of free inquiry and critical judgment it has encouraged people to study religion and to study it seriously. In fact, a religious revival is on its way to China.

Within the Christian church there is a rapidly developing consciousness of a Chinese church. The desire for an indigenous church which does not sever its continuity from the historic churches of the West, but takes full cognizance of the spiritual and racial inheritance of the Chinese people, has become the rallying point of many Christians. Along with it there is the insistent desire for a more thorough understanding and more adequate interpretation of Christian teaching, and a more effective application of it to social and individual life. From every part of the country Christians are yearning for better preachers, better Christian literature and a more thorough Christian programme. Among the missionary workers in the field there have been an increasing number of people who have enlarged the scope of Christian missionary endeavour, and have come to appreciate the necessity of restating the missionary aim, so as to make it more comprehensive and more effective in meeting the needs of the people whom they have been loyally serving. Beginnings have been made toward greater efficiency in missionary service through union and fuller co-operation. Such new qualities combined with the growing consciousness of the Chinese church itself promise great development.

As we look forward into the future we see many problems ahead of us in industrial development, in economic change and in the disintegration of the family-system as the result of the various forces at work. China is at the cross-roads. Is she heading towards full emancipation and progress or to narrow and one-sided development and confusion ? Shall China go through all the mistakes and the travail of Western nations in her next few decades of transformation or shall she be able to profit by their experience ?

There is no time more critical and yet more full of promise. There is no time when consultation and co-operation on the part of Christian leaders is more urgently needed to make their contributions to the salvation of the nation—a nation which includes one-fourth of the human race.

II

CHINA'S RENAISSANCE

By TIMOTHY TINGFANG LEW,

Acting Dean, Faculty of Theology, Yen Ching University, Peking

I. WHAT IS CHINA'S RENAISSANCE?

CAREFUL students of oriental history will have noticed that there are four important stages through which China has gone in the last hundred years. The great empire, isolated from the rest of the world on account of its geographical limitations, began to have its barriers broken down through modern steamships, and the sleeping giant was rudely awakened by the naval powers of the west. About the middle of the nineteenth century the Chinese people began to take serious notice of the scientific and military powers of western nations. They gradually realised that there was something which the western nations possessed and they themselves did not have. This change of opinion toward the West began the movement for introducing modern mechanical science. From that time on until the last decade of the nineteenth century, a period of forty years, several leading statesmen did all they

could to overcome prejudices, and started the
building of arsenals and shipyards and a navy, and
the translating of western books related to these
forms of activity. The change was gradual, but
nevertheless significant. A perusal of the writings
of scholars and memorials to the throne by pro-
gressive officials, and the papers written by the
candidates for Government examinations will show
that there was an increasing number of people, year
after year, whose attention was directed toward the
movement for introducing that which in their sight
made the Western nations strong.

Then came the war with Japan, with its defeat.
A second change began its operation, for people
began to realise that it was not merely guns and
battleships and such mechanical devices that
represented the source of Western power. More
than a navy, guns and machinery, was needed—the
men behind the guns, the minds that control the
navy, and skilful hands to operate the machinery.
Thus, attention was shifted from the outward
scientific mechanisms toward the training of men to
meet the scientific demand, and the movement for
New Learning became popular. The old examination system was to be abolished and a new educational system to be introduced, but this important
movement was frustrated by the coup d'etat of
1898, with its subsequent reaction of 1900, which
put China in a very awkward situation politically.

When the nation passed through the excruciating pains of the Boxer struggle, the third change was brought about, for people began to see that without a new system of government there could be very little progress along the line of education. Thus the people directed their attention to the reformation of the government. Some directed their efforts toward the attainment of a constitutional, monarchical form of government; but others joined the ranks of those working for a revolution, which resulted in the overthrow of the monarchy and the establishment of The Republic.

Since 1911, the people have been led to see that a mere change of government, while it has brought many boons and freed people from many evils that are inherent in the monarchical form of absolute control, is not enough, and that the secret of the strength of a country and the regenerate life of a nation has to come through a more far reaching change than that of a change of governmental system. The time was ripe for the fourth change, the change of point of view, a movement for a change in the philosophy of life.

This movement is a logical sequence of a series of past changes. It burst into bloom like a glorious flower whose bud, protecting leaves, twigs and root can be traced without much difficulty, though its beauty and richness crown the whole process of growth and startle the onlooker. To this movement

we shall give the name of " China's Renaissance,"
and in this short article we shall endeavour to give
a few of its important aspects and its significance,
not only for the Chinese people themselves, but also
for the world.

II. What are the predominant notes of emphasis ?

We call this movement " China's Renaissance "
because, first of all it is a movement primarily of
learning. It has its nursery in some of the leading
higher institutions of the land, and the people who
were immediately connected with the movement and
who have rendered the most significant service are
the university and college professors and the
students.

Second, this is a movement of many sided
interests, touching the life of society and the life of
the individual at many points.

Third, it is a movement which advocates a more
ardent study of things Chinese, of all things ancient,
literature, history and philosophy, but by the
application of new methods of research.

Fourth, this is a movement which welcomes
everything new from whatever source.

Fifth, this is a movement which centres its
interest around man—man in the present world,
man in this life, and aims at the improvement of the
well-being of man and to hasten its progress.

Sixth, this is a movement which places a peculiar emphasis upon art, besides its emphasis on literature.

The movement in Chinese is usually known as the " *Hsing Wen Hua Yuan Tung*," which literally translated would be " *The New Civilisation Movement*," for its hope is to recast the old civilisation and to build up a new one. Taking the movement as a whole, we will note that there are certain predominant points of emphasis.

First, there is the emphasis upon science : science of every kind, and science in its various aspects, is emphasised. Science as a method is strongly advocated and persistently followed. Before its sceptre all authorities, ancient and modern, must pass in review. Nothing is to be accepted unless it can stand the tests of the scientific method.

Second, there is an equal emphasis upon democracy. The movement has been a relentless foe to despotic government and autocratic institutions of every sort. Its work is a searchlight to expose the faults and weaknesses of the systems that are undemocratic. It causes their shortcomings to stare in the faces of the people. It stirs up men's reason against them, and it pushes on like a mighty force to fight against them.

Third, there is the emphasis upon social reform. The movement has been increasing in the intensity of its social point of view. Different from all past movements, it calls the attention of the people to the fact that since it is the people who constitute the nation, it is the people who sustain the government. No reformation of government could effectively be made by merely changing the political organisation. If there is any hope for a reform at all, it must begin with the people. Social problems in their technical sense therefore become the fundamental problems, and a social point of view becomes the all-embracing point of view. The movement is seriously discussing how to reconstruct the family system, how to mitigate the sufferings of the people, and particularly of those people who belong to the so-called socially inferior strata. The problem of labour and capital, the problem of non-employment, the problem of divorce and all the problems that are related to social improvement have taken the centre of interest.

In the fourth place, the movement lays the emphasis upon relentless thoroughness. The movement has thus far proved to be one which has unusual courage and persistency. No obstacle is too great to overcome, and no compromise is small enough to be tolerated. It does not rest satisfied with any temporary shiftwork or patchwork, it aims at a thorough-going change, if anything needs change at all. So, there is nothing too radical for examination. Conventions and traditions have lost their prestige. Time-honoured practices, if in any way they do not meet the exigencies of the present day, are to be cast aside, root and branch, altogether. Proprieties and customs which have ruled for centuries, give way unless they can withstand the challenge that is being put to them. The movement does not hesitate to overturn every stone in the social structure if in doing so it sees the promise of a new and better structure.

III. WHAT ARE ITS CHIEF ACTIVITIES ?

With these main emphases the movement has carried on, or rather expressed itself in many forms of activity, a few of which are worthy of special attention.

First, its leaders are working for a thorough reform of the Chinese written language. The vast territory of China, embracing 400,000,000 inhabitants, owing to its geographical structure and its insufficient transport facilities, has gradually developed a number of dialects, which while fundamentally similar in syntax and word construction, are different in pronunciation and in many cases in the expressions used. But the nation was united under the one system of the written language, which, though pronounced differently when read according to the variations of the different dialects, yet carries the same meaning and is uniformly understood throughout the country. But this written language has a history of several thousand years. It has been developed and over-developed in its intricacy, in its beauty and richness. Its relation to the spoken language is very similar to that which existed between Latin and the various spoken vernaculars of European nations a few centuries ago. It does not require much effort for the average student of history to realise the inconveniences which were experienced by the peoples of Europe a few centuries back when all learning was perpetuated through Latin, and how the different vernaculars of the various nations gradually shook off the bondage of Latin, and made for themselves worthy places in the evolution of European civilisation. Now, China has just been facing the same difficulty. All education is carried on with the classical style of writing as its medium. It is a beautiful and precious heritage of the race, but it is not a convenient tool for an age in which education must be made democratic and within the reach of every citizen. The Renaissance Movement in China, therefore, has concentrated its effort in the last three or four years on fighting for a place for that which is known as the *conversational style of writing*. This, hitherto, has been confined to the writing of certain novels and has never been regarded as the language of polite writing. But it has the advantage over the classical style in its directness, in its simplicity and in the closeness to the everyday conversational vernacular. The effort of enthroning this style of writing in the place of the classical style has been nothing short of a terrific war waged between the scholars—a multitude of scholars on the one hand and a handful of leaders of the new movement on the other. But the latter have won the war. They have been consistently urging upon the nation that everything must be written in this colloquial style, for it is only by doing so that we can shake off the shackles of the undemocratic ideas which through their representatives were the patrons of the classical style. The old classical style has been moulded and shaped to show the differences of the higher and the lower, the ruler and the ruled. It was made difficult so that it could not be a handy tool for the common people. It has also been imbued with the superstitions of the ages, thus making it unfit as a category to be employed by men of science.

This work is very fundamental for in it all the points of emphasis of the movement find their concrete expression : scientific methods, democratic principles, social idealism and thorough-going reconstruction. This work has been justifying itself because it has given people a new tool for expression. The conversational style has been steadily improving itself in diction, in clearness, in brevity and other fine qualities. It has also revolutionised poetical writings. Free verse has been introduced which has liberated the inarticulate thought and feeling of many inspired hearts.

Second, the movement has been working hard in introducing the literature of foreign nations. China has been engaged in translating foreign books for years, but always with two defects. First, there has been the defect in selection. The selection has been rather narrow and along certain lines and the choice has been largely superficial. Second, the translations have been rendered in the old classical style. The new wines were put into old bottles with the result that both were spoiled. This movement with its effective tool of expression in the conversational style has remedied the second of these two defects and with remarkable rapidity it has introduced into China all kinds of Western writings which possess fundamental significance. One will be surprised to find the kind of subjects that are being discussed in the Chinese magazines and books and daily newspapers, and the points of view expressed and theories advocated therein. The movement has, therefore, also remedied the first of the two defects, the one of superficiality and narrowness in the choice of books to be translated, and of theories to be imparted and of topics to be discussed. One can pick out from any bookstore a score of magazines and books in which one finds the same kind of subject matter as one would find in any assorted collection of magazines and books to be found in the bookstores of London, New York, Paris or Berlin.

Third, the movement has started the systematic research of the Chinese civilisation of the past. The vast amount of philosophical writings which have hitherto been left in unorganised form are now being systematically reduced in order and being put within the reach of the understanding of the average student. Canonical writings of ancient sages, writings which have been held in awe and reverence, to be memorised and to be revered and not to be criticised or scrutinised, are now being put through the rigid test of higher and lower criticism. They are examined and evaluated, and interpreted for the average mind. The most popular books include the volumes of the *History of Ancient Chinese Philosophy*, *History of the Thought of the Manchu Dynasty*, and books of a like interest. The application of scientific methods of historical criticism, the liberation from slavish obedience to the past, the new interest in social reformation and the undaunted courage with which thoroughness is aimed at, these combined are giving new impetus to the study of things Chinese and the treasures of China's past.

Fourth, the movement has encouraged the organisation of groups and societies, local and national, to study the various problems in a democratic and open way. One can hardly make a complete list of the various organisations that are springing up in various quarters throughout the land, emphasising one aspect or another of the movement, and encouraging the study of one social problem or another. Some of these are naturally short-lived, but there are quite a few which are full of promise for an important future. The movement has developed a habit among people, and particularly among students, of being dissatisfied with existing conditions. It encourages them to study present-day problems with all seriousness and with all the facilities within their reach. To mention just a few names :—"Society to Discuss Family Reconstruction," "Science Society," "Society for Promoting New Education," "Philosophical Society," "Marxian Society," will suffice to show us the varieties and the breadth of the interest this movement represents.

Fifth, the movement has given birth to several hundred new periodicals, weeklies, monthlies, quarterlies and annuals. My last census, which was naturally incomplete because made last winter, showed that there were over two hundred periodicals, all written in the conversational style, and discussing all kinds of problems, from Civic Liberty to Communism, Women's Education to Birth Control, and from an Interpretation of Dante to Criticism of Dostoievsky. The number of periodicals is still increasing, although some of them have been outlived by others, and it will be not only surprising but also really interesting for a Westerner to see some of the magazines which may include in a single issue a complete play by Hauptmann, Maeterlink, Bjornsen, or Oscar Wilde. In the same volume one may find an abstract of the philosophy of Bergson, a discussion on Eucken, a criticism of Bertrand Russell, and the review of a book by John Dewey. New terms are being created and new expressions introduced which dazzle the reader's eyes and create hunger for some study in order to get further explanation.

Sixth, the movement has been crystallising the efforts of various leading organisations that promote learning and some of the higher institutions to invite western scholars to lecture in China. There has been organised in Peking the society known as " The Society for Lectures on New Learning," patronised by distinguished publicists and co-operated in by the National Universities and Colleges. The society with its co-operators has been instrumental in bringing over to China several of the world's leading scholars. John Dewey of America was the first one thus honoured. Bertrand Russell followed. Driesch and Bergson are expected to come in the near future and plans have been under way to invite other scholars from Europe and America. Those who are interested in education also organised what is known as " The Educational Survey Society." Paul Monroe of America has been invited to make a thorough and critical survey of the present-day education of China. All these societies are supported by voluntary contributions and the approval and co-operation of the leading scholars, educationists, and publicists of China. The visiting scholars have found a hearty welcome everywhere they went, and whatever they had to present was eagerly examined and carefully scrutinised. The works of these scholars find considerable sale in their original languages in China and translations into Chinese are being rapidly turned out. The conservative publishers in some cases have been surprised at the good sale of these books, seemingly obscure and difficult to understand. One illustration will suffice. When Bertrand Russell was lecturing in Peking, an arrangement was made to take down his lectures verbatim and a special monthly was published, known as *The Russell Monthly*. The first issue was to be 6,000 copies. The publisher undertook the order with reserved distrust, but later on confided to the editor of the monthly that he never dreamed that 6,000 copies were not enough and that further editions would actually be in demand.

IV. What is it accomplishing?

Any discerning reader will gain from the discussion thus far an idea of what importance the movement has with all these emphases and activities. The movement in its definite expression is only a few years old. One needs perhaps to reserve his judgment as to its future, but one cannot be blind to the effect which it already has produced, however uneven it may be in various places. Only a few of the outstanding points of importance will be enumerated.

First, it has been revolutionising the thinking of the students. The movement has worked upon the mental isolation of the people as previous movements have acted upon the geographical isolation of the nation. One after another, the closed doors have been broken open and impassable barriers removed. The oriental horizon of the people, particularly of the students, is being steadily expanded. They see problems which did not exist for them before. They acquire points of view which were beyond them in the past. They are given categories in which to think, which were not at their disposal in days gone by, and they are being drilled in new methods of using their thinking capacity. They are given the freedom to think as they see fit and as the situation demands. They do not have to bow down before ancient authorities which have controlled their thoughts and the thoughts of their ancestors for generations.

Second, it is giving birth to a rational and better balanced national consciousness. All students of China have noticed the development and growth of national consciousness in China in the last few decades, but a careful analysis will find that it has gone through various stages. There was, first, the stage in which the nation was rudely shocked by foreign invasions, but comforted itself in its past greatness and the blind confidence in its past power to overcome all difficulties. Then, it went through the stage which was characterised by reactions born out of the desperate situations involved in its efforts to check foreign aggression. Such efforts resulted in anything but improvement of the situation. The nation then went through the third stage, which was characterised by a kind of discouragement which magnified the helplessness of the situation, coupled with timid confusion, undue recognition of the strength of modern powers, and a stoic resignation toward existing conditions as unavoidable. The movement came at this critical stage to awaken in the hearts of the people new courage and hope. It points out the way for reformation and for change, however difficult and gigantic the task may be. It teaches the people not to be discouraged simply because the problem is difficult, by pointing out to them that each nation has its own difficult problems. It teaches the people to be neither the slaves nor the scoffers of the past, but to study the past with a fresh insight, for it believes that the Chinese race with its history of 5,000 years has a valuable spiritual inheritance which being properly interpreted will furnish a great deal of that which China needs to-day. It teaches the people neither prejudice against things foreign nor the acceptance of them without reserve, but to learn from other nations as a humble disciple the things which China does not possess in equal measure, and to strive to make contributions to other nations as she should. In the last few years, one can notice that the educational efforts in China have been centred around a desperate fight to overthrow that idea of nationalism which has been imported from Japan—a narrow, self-centred, selfish nationalism, and replace it by a well-balanced, democratic nationalism such as is demonstrated by the better part of the democratic nations of the west and reinforced by the peace-loving nature of the Chinese people.

Third, it has inaugurated a nation-wide tendency to progress. The movement has made people acquire a wholesome dissatisfaction with existing conditions. Such dissatisfaction has been most difficult to develop among people who have a great past to revere, and who have deeply ingrained habits due to the long life of the nation. Both of these factors have inevitably led the people into self-satisfaction, and on the top of this there also come the economic stringency due to a great population. All these combined to create an inertia both in the individual and in the nation against the adoption of things new and against the continual effort necessary after renewal. This movement has " hit the mark." It creates dissatisfaction and it does more than that.

It helps to make every dissatisfaction more specific and concrete, it constantly reminds people that such dissatisfaction can only be ended by putting forth proper efforts, adopting right methods, and reinforcing these with persistence. Nothing is too new to be discussed in China to-day, and nothing too radical for experiment. Given opportunities, one is reasonably sure that in a few years many experiments, social and political, may be made. Thorough-going changes will be put into actual practice, for this movement will not rest satisfied with any temporary amelioration of the sufferings and difficulties ; it has in it the seed of perpetual life, pushing on and on.

Fourth, the importance of the movement can further be noticed by its ability to permeate the whole fabric of the nation. The movement began with the university professors and students, and it is now rapidly trickling through the various strata of society. Books and periodicals are being read by various kinds of people. New ideas are invading families of even the most conservative sort. Authorities are shattered in various quarters. Many changes that are going on may not clearly and definitely be credited to this movement, yet, nevertheless, they are being fed by the inspiration and encouragement of this movement. It is a significant fact that in this movement it is neither the leaders nor the formal organisations that figure the most.

In fact, the movement takes upon its own shoulders as one of its tasks the dethroning of every idol, and it makes no attempt to establish any nation-wide formal organisation or to state any definite platform. The pervading atmosphere which it creates everywhere, the subtler influence which works upon the minds of thinking people, and its persuasive ability to encourage people to make a right-about turn, these constitute the power of the movement ; and, what is more, its tenacity in clinging to whatever quarter it is invading, is bound to make the influence of the movement permanent wherever it takes root.

Fifth, and what is most important of all, it is leading people on to search for a new philosophy of life. The movement has again and again brought people back to the fundamental question, " What is life ? " and " What is the philosophy of life ? " Young and old, men and women, teachers and students, are inquiring into this fundamental question. They have discussed the problem. They have debated over it. They have written on it, and some of them have died for it. Thus far, the movement has told people that the rational life, following the principles of science, working for the social improvement of the whole with eyes wide open to the problems of the present—this constitutes the gist of the best philosophy of life. It is very noteworthy that the attitude of the movement towards religion is immature, dogmatic and one-sided, and yet full of promise. This leads me to the next main topic, the effect of the movement upon religious life.

V. WHAT IS ITS SIGNIFICANCE FOR THE RELIGIOUS LIFE OF THE PEOPLE ?

Any thorough-going discussion of this problem will naturally be an elaborate one. Elsewhere* I have presented the various aspects of the attitude of the movement toward religion in general and Christianity in particular, and its effects upon Christianity in general in China. Space only permits of the barest outline. Here the outstanding views with regard to religion are of the following kinds :—

First, some challenge the necessity of religion in a world of science.

Second, some emphasise the fact that religion needs more adequate interpretation and assistance from philosophy.

Third, some urge the purification of religion from superstition and dogmatic beliefs and despotic control.

Fourth, some advocate the substitution of aesthetics for religion because the former contains all the values which religion possesses.

Fifth, some doubt that religion offers any benefit at all that is unmixed with evil and whether the game is worth the candle.

* Chinese Recorder, May, 1921, pub. in Shanghai, China.

Sixth, some believe that it is possible as well as desirable to obtain all the values such as spirit and courage and faith, and to claim the products of religion, without accepting religion itself.

Seventh, some point out the fact that religion is indispensable because no human being can escape the four inevitable facts of life—birth, sickness, age, and death.

This, roughly and briefly, represents the various views on the subject of religion which have been predominant in this movement.

VI. WHAT SIGNIFICANCE HAS IT FOR CHRISTIANITY IN CHINA ?

For us Christians the problem that is of tremendous interest is the attitude of the movement toward Christianity, with some of its effects.

First of all, the movement challenges the place of Christianity in individual and national life, for, if the existence of any religion is in question, Christianity cannot alone escape the same tests. Is Christianity really a mere concomitant of the backwardness of civilisation, and absence of science, and an incomplete philosophy ? If so, shall China continue to be contented, like the rest of the world, with the existing conditions of the past which made religion more or less useful ? Or, shall China work for a better civilisation and a greater progress in science and a more reliable philosophy rather than accept provisionally a temporary relief through religion ? Or, if she chooses such temporary relief, should that religion be Christianity ?

Second, the movement encourages the study of Christianity. Christianity has in China passed through three stages. The first stage was one of pure prejudice on account of its being something newly introduced by foreigners. Then it went through a stage of contempt for its alleged crudity and inadequate presentation, owing to the difficulties involved in using the Chinese language and understanding the Chinese people and thought on the part of the missionaries.

Then we come to the third stage, the stage of indifference, an indifference which closed the door more tightly than either prejudice or contempt. This indifference is now being removed by this movement. For the very principle of this movement forbids indifference, to say nothing of prejudice. Christianity does constitute a problem of society ; it is a problem of the people, and it is also a problem of the philosophy of life. At the very least it is a problem ! And as such it deserves a critical examination before we pronounce our verdict of rejection or acceptance. For this very reason Christianity is finding people who are paying it earnest attention as a subject worthy of study and discussion in circles and among individuals where Christianity never had a chance of being heard heretofore.

Third, this movement is making way for Christianity. Both Christianity and this movement have found a common foe in the existing superstitions, whether in the life of the individual or of society. Much of the work of Christianity has been fighting against superstitions which were the products of ignorance. The ignorance may be due to a lack of scientific knowledge of the natural world or due to the lack of critical insight into the spiritual life. Christianity has been waging an incessant war in the last century, ever since her arrival upon the soil of China, against idolatrous worship, the trust in pseudo-scientific astrology, popular trust in distorted practices based upon certain relics of half-understood philosophy, and many other similar beliefs and practices, parallels to which historians could easily find in the history of European peoples in former ages. Christianity has fought these wars almost single-handed. Now this movement is fighting against the very same enemies and with even greater relentlessness. By its very tenet of accepting nothing unless it is critically examined and proven to be worthy of acceptance, it has knocked down and shattered many an idol which has held sway over the people and which Christianity has often failed to root out as completely as she wanted to.

Fourth, this movement has directly or indirectly given recognition to Christian work. It is only blind prejudice or unscientific partiality which could make one deny the various contributions, however limited they may be in scope, which Christianity has made towards the social progress of China in the last fifty years. The fight which Christians waged against the evil of opium is a notable one. The fact that the opium was introduced into China at the point of the bayonet by a Christian nation often overshadows the heroic fight Christians put up through all these years. The introduction of free medical service according to modern scientific practices has another notable record. One can mention other items which have directly or indirectly contributed to social progress or which have led others to work for that end. But these good works of Christians have been given very little proper recognition, simply because they were under Christian auspices ; to the average mind it was taken as a necessary part of the scheme of propaganda. The real significance of social service as an expression of Christian faith and the real motive power which is behind all these Christian social services have not been properly understood. This movement with its increasing emphasis upon social progress and humanitarianism has opened the eyes of the people to see the real value and proper motive of social service. The *raison d'être* of various forms of Christian activities is gradually being understood and the simple notion of regarding all Christian social service as a mere scheme of propaganda with ulterior motives is gradually passing away.

Fifth, as a natural consequence, this movement promises the possibility of increasing popular support to Christian work. One is not ready to say that this movement will lead people to accept the Christian faith and help them to bear the Christian yoke of service, but through its continual instruction there will be more people who appreciate social service and who will acquire some of the fundamentals required in the carrying on of any form of social service. The people will be better prepared to respond to any Christian call for social betterment. They will, at least, understand what Christians are trying to do. One can thus within a safe limit prophesy that, if this movement should go on without wavering from its social principle, it will give indirect and even direct support to genuine Christian work. Indications of this kind are already not lacking. " Anti-bad-habit societies," " Social service clubs," " Free Schools for the children of the poor," conducted by volunteers and many other similar activities are being organised by students all over the country, and in the large centres these societies and organisations have proved their readiness to co-operate with similar societies and organisations founded under Christian auspices. Christian theology may not attract the students, but Christian expressions of social service have furnished a common ground upon which all forces can unite.

Sixth, the most important effect which this movement has upon Christianity and the students' life is to be found in the creative work of the conversational style of the written language which has been described above. Christianity came to China out and out as the gospel for the poor, the gospel for the ignorant, and the gospel for those who are in darkness. The Bible was translated into the vernacular as well as into the classical written language, but the predominant usage in the Christian church throughout the century was the vernacular of the Holy Scriptures, and most of its tracts and books were written in the vernacular. For this reason Christianity was looked down upon and suffered seriously at the hands of the public. There was very little respect for Christianity because the obtrusiveness due to its strangeness was aggravated by its undue simplicity. It was regarded as a religion beneath the attention of the elite and the cultured. But Christianity held on its way unwaveringly. This movement has suddenly declared to the people that the ancient classical language, the beautiful, the elegant, the difficult-to-understand, the polite, was also the high-brow, the autocratic, the undemocratic, the anti-social, unfit for citizens of a republic. That which is to be honoured because it is useful, because it is good for the many, because it is within reach of all, because it can be acquired in a much shorter time, is the very vernacular which they have despised. It points out the fact that they despised the vernacular simply because they were fooled by the autocrats who used the difficulty of the classical language to keep knowledge from the people and to make their own position look more dignified. Students of to-day, while studying the classical language in institutions of higher learning have made an almost right-about turn in their attitude toward the vernacular, and the kind of vernacular which they are adopting and developing, whose style and beauty they are creating, is very near to the type of vernacular which has been used, advocated, and taught in the Christian church. What a tremendous change of opinion this involves one can hardly realise in its fullness.

Seventh, this change in the problem of literature brings about a latent possibility of revival in Christian learning because the effect of this change is beneficial in a mutual way. Not only the non-Christians have thereby acquired a better and more correct attitude toward the Christian literature, but also the Christian students themselves have begun to realise how much there is to be done in improving the vernacular which has been in vogue in the Christian Church heretofore. For this movement not only aims at using the vernacular as a tool for expression, but is also trying to make the vernacular a basis for a new literature not less elegant or less effective than the ancient classical language Christian students are therefore urged to work for a better and more perfect vernacular, in which to present Christian faith and Christian thought, to interpret Christian experience, and to express Christian aspirations. Under such pressure of encouragement one can confidently look forward to the production of an amount of new Christian literature, more expressive, more beautiful, and more worthy of its content.

Eighth, there will be also a deepening and enrichment of Christian experience and Christian faith among the students who are already Christians in China. No intelligent Christian student who is not out of touch with the currents of the time can be free from the healthy influence of this movement. The very inquiring attitude and critical temper with which this movement has filled the atmosphere affects also the Christian students and produces revolutionary effects upon their faith. They begin to ask questions, they begin to search for the whys and wherefores of every Christian doctrine and ecclesiastical practice. Their views of the Bible are being put through a hot crucible. People begin to be interested in the formation of the canons of the Old and New Testaments and in the origins of Christian traditions, and to appraise the values of orthodoxy. With proper guidance such a self-initiative activity of mind can produce very valuable contributions to the Christian life of the individual students and through them to the Christian life of the Church as a whole.

VII. WHAT IS ITS RELATION TO THE WORLD BROTHERHOOD OF STUDENTS ?

One can see even at a glance what bearing the effects produced by this movement upon the students of China have upon the brotherhood of students throughout the world, for there are several points of great importance that deserve the attention of this brotherhood.

First of all, we may note the very significant fact that the interests of students in China from now on are becoming identical with the interests of students throughout the world. The problems which interest the Chinese students are the very problems which are of interest to the students of other nations. They admire, they scoff at, they criticise, they worship the same group of savants, philosophers, scientists, heroes, and martyrs. As fast as new theories are being advanced and made known in other nations they are discussed by the students in their publications and in their forums. With the increasing facility for translation, new books are being translated which guide and direct the attention of Chinese students along the same channels through which the thoughts of the students of other nations are moving.

Second, we should note the more significant fact that the Chinese students are not only interested in the same problems as those in which the students of other nations are interested, but they are also thinking on these same problems in the same categories and using the same terms. This is going on in two ways. First, the translation of the terms and categories from foreign languages into Chinese, and second, there is an increasing number of students studying foreign languages. The latest deliberations of the National Educational Association in China, representing every province of the Republic, recorded in its new programme for national education the requirement that every student going through the college or university should learn at least two foreign languages. This shows the trend of the times. In education, in politics, in commerce, and in every line of thought, the students are brought into contact as far as the conditions permit, with the latest and most popular categories of thinking in foreign nations. The rapidity with which the Chinese students absorb these and make them their own has been very noteworthy.

Third, there is a still more important fact, more important than the interest in the same problems, more important than thinking in the same categories, and that is the setting up of the same aims and the cherishing of the same hopes. Take, for instance, international brotherhood and universal peace. What higher aim and what more blessed hope can one entertain ? The Chinese students even in these critical hours of their national destiny, facing internal difficulties and external aggression, are still working for the same high aim and fostering the same high hope which the very best students throughout the world are working for and cherishing. They are trying their best to take the sting out of the hardship which China is suffering under the international injustices of the last few years by keeping alive their faith in the final victory of justice and righteousness. Against the very enemies which are encroaching upon the sovereignty and blighting the future of their country they are using not the weapon of blind hatred, but the solemn warning that the righteous forces for universal world brotherhood ultimately shall triumph. It is very significant that this movement while stirring up the nation by reminding the students day after day that unless they fight a decisive battle for a regenerated nation there is no hope for China, yet through the same mouthpiece has never failed to preach the gospel of the brotherhood of men throughout the world.

There are other hopes and there are other aims, expressed or unexpressed, held by the students of other nations which are finding echoes and spiritual responses among the Chinese students. The same successes inspire the students of China and the students of other nations, and the same failures dishearten them equally.

VIII. WHAT HOPES DOES THIS MOVEMENT INSPIRE?

Facing the tremendous power of this unprecedented movement, shall we as the members of the student brotherhood of the world not confidently hope for great results?

First of all, shall we not hope that the Chinese students in going through this process of mental revolution in their growing contact with the minds of the West, will profit not only by the passing thoughts of the West, but also by the actual experience of this rapidly moving age? The students of the West and the people of the West in general are going through many experiments and tests. Their successes and failures, their bitterness and joys can all be of tremendous value to the Chinese students, so that in the process of social, national and racial transformation the Chinese people should not have to go through all the profitless and misdirected ways of the past. They need not begin where the Western nations started, but where the latter left off.

Second, shall we not also hope that the students of China, with the rich heritage of a noble past, and with fine innate qualities recognised by all impartial students of the world, in going through the process of restudying the wisdom of the sages and reinterpreting the spiritual inheritance of their race, reappraising the value of their 5,000 years of national experience, may make such contributions as will not only be beacon lights to themselves but also to the world ?

Third, when these two processes are going on can we not find a surer ground for hope of a genuine and lasting internationalism—an internationalism that is based not on treaties and covenants which can be torn up at any time as mere scraps of paper, an internationalism which is based not upon clever interpretations of carefully worded promises which can be manipulated and twisted in the hands of knaves as the very weapon to destroy its own life, but an internationalism based upon the unity of interest, unity of thought, unity of aims and hopes, and unity of hearts.

The students of China are ready.   What will the students of other nations do ?

January, 1922.
   Peking.

III

THE LITERARY REVOLUTION IN CHINA
By Hu Shih (Suh Hu)

Professor of Literature, National University, Peking

In order to appreciate the full significance of the literary revolution in China, the reader will do well by recalling the history of the rise of the national languages of modern Europe. Hardly five centuries have passed since Latin was the recognised literary language of whole Europe. Italy was the first to revolt. Dante, Petrarch (in his youthful days), and Boccaccio produced their best works in the dialect of Tuscany, and the popularity of their writings succeeded in finally making the Tuscan dialect the national language of the Italian people. By that time, the dialect of Paris was fast becoming the official language of France. In 1539, Francis I. ordered that all public documents should be in the French of Paris, though it was still foreign to nearly half of the population in the kingdom. In the middle of the sixteenth century, there arose the group of French poets known as the *Pléiade*, who consciously advocated the use of the French language as a means of poetic expression. Rabelais and Montaigne achieved an even greater success in prose. Thus by the end of the sixteenth century the French of Paris became the undisputed national language of France.

The case of modern English, being more similar to that of modern Chinese, is all the more instructive. As late as the latter part of the fourteenth century, there were three main dialects competing for supremacy in England. The Southern dialect, spoken south of the Thames, was the most conservative, being full of old forms and inflections. The Northern dialect which extended from the Humber to Aberdeen, was, owing to the Danish settlements, undergoing such rapid and radical changes that it became almost an entirely new language. Between these two extremes stood the Midland dialect which was more or less comprehensible to the speakers of both dialects. This Midland dialect, being the language of London and of the two great universities, soon came to be adopted as the standard speech. Chaucer, the greatest poet of the fourteenth century, wrote his poetry in this dialect ; and his great contemporary, Wycliff, too, used it in his English translations of the Bible. The immense popularity of their writings and the introduction of the printing press in the following century made the Midland dialect the undisputed national tongue of England.

The lesson taught by such recent history seems to have been forgotten by those who now look upon the Chinese literary revolution with disfavour and suspicion. But a little unbiased reflection and historical study will readily lead us to the conclusion that what is now called the literary revolution is no more than a culminating stage in a long process of historical evolution.

The story is indeed a long one, but the salient facts are simple. As early as the second century B.C., the classical language had already become unintelligible to the people. Thus about the year 120 B.C., in a memorial to the emperor, Premier Kung-sun Hung said : " The imperial edicts and laws that have been proclaimed, . . . while they are most elegantly worded and containing benevolent instructions, are not generally understood by the public officers who are too inadequately educated to explain these to the people." In order to meet this most serious difficulty the government hit upon a system under which public offices were conferred upon those who had studied the classic writings. This system, which was later perfected into the great system of literary examinations, has succeeded in maintaining to this day the supremacy of the classical language, which had become unintelligible to the public officers over two thousand years ago.

But no governmental power, however great, can prevent language from undergoing the inevitable processes of phonetical change and grammatical levelling gradually and unconsciously brought about by the common sense of the people. In China, these processes by a stroke of good fortune have been allowed to go on unimpeded and uninterfered with by the literary class which was busily occupied with the task of mastering the subtleties of the dead classical language. For a long period of over twenty centuries, the dialects have been permitted to keep on changing and modifying until some of the dialects have become as distinct from the classical language as any two cognate languages can possibly be different from each other. As in the case of the English dialects, the dialects of Northern China, owing to the influence of numerous barbarian conquests and settlements, have undergone the most radical changes both in pronunciation and intonation and in grammar. It is the Northern and Middle dialects, generally classed as the " Mandarin dialects," which now form the *kuo yu*, or national language of China.

While conservative Chinese scholars still look down upon the living spoken language as the degraded jargon of the vulgar and the illiterate, the student of comparative languages can easily convince himself that the living national tongue is the culmination of over twenty centuries' linguistic revision and reform, and is consequently by far superior to the long dead classical language. I have elsewhere tried to prove this point by numerous illustrations,* but the

* Hu Shih, *Selected Writings*, vol. III., pp. 1-80. Also Hu Shih, *The National Language of China*, in a volume to be published by the American University Club of Shanghai.

limitations of this paper do not allow me to take up a subject of such technical nature. So I shall confine myself to the development of literature in the spoken language.

The first barbarisation of Northern China, which took place during the fourth, fifth, and sixth centuries A.D., and its concomitant event of the shift of the centre of Chinese civilisation to Southern China—these two factors combined to produce a large number of popular poems both in the North and in the South. The new races in the North made their heroic and warlike songs, but the popular literature of the southern peoples chiefly consisted in little lyrics of love. The unmistakable beauty and simplicity of these songs of the people gradually came to be appreciated by the literary men of the time and they soon became models of poetic composition under the general name of *Ku yo fu*, or Old Songs. In this way the literature of the literati was influenced by the poetry of the people, and the greatness of the poetry of the Tang dynasty (620-900) owes much to the influence of the popular songs of the pre-Tang period. It is safe to say that the best poems of Tang are written either in the popular tongue or in a style nearest to it. It is said of Po Chu-I, the greatest poet of the Mid-Tang period, that his poems were often shown to an old woman, whose inability to understand a certain poem would cause its rejection or revision.

It was also under the Tang dynasty that vulgate prose first arose. The great teachers of the *Chuan* or *Zen* School of Buddhism first used it in preaching and recording sayings and discourses. The style proved to be so effective in philosophical writings that the Neo-Confucian philosophers of Sung and later dynasties had to adopt it in most of their philosophical discussions.

Meanwhile Northern China was undergoing a second period of barbarization which began in the tenth century and lasted until the latter part of the fourteenth. The Kitan Tartars were conquered by the Luchen Tartars, who in turn were conquered by the Mongols. The latter people in the year 1239 succeeded in subjugating the whole of China. While these barbarian conquests were politically and socially disastrous to the Chinese people, it cannot be denied that they have had immense beneficial effects upon the language and literature of the people. That the language was barbarized can be easily seen in the numerous edicts and other public documents of the Mongol dynasty, which have been preserved to us and which were all written in terribly barbarized Chinese, in a style which is apparently Mongol syntax clothed in Chinese characters.

It was during this period of barbarian occupation that the great dramas were produced. The literary examinations were suspended for nearly

in the middle of the eighteenth century. Aside
from the effects of their outspoken attacks on Chinese
officialdom, these modern novels are significant in
the fact that, while they were all written in the
Mandarin dialect, their authors were all southerners
to whom the northern and middle dialects were not
at all native. This fact shows the tremendous
educative effects of the great novels which have in
the course of a few centuries succeeded in standard-
ising the national language and have been its greatest
teachers and propagandists.

From the above account, it is clear that spoken
Chinese as represented by the Mandarin dialects is
well qualified to become the national language of
China. In the first place, it is the most widely
spoken language in the country. In the second place
it has produced a vast amount of literature, a
literature more extensive and varied than any
modern European language ever possessed at the
time of its establishment as a national language.
It seems incredible that a language of such vitality
and currency should have to wait so long before it
was ever thought of as a possible substitute for the
long dead classical language. But the explanation
is really simple. The authority of the classical
language and literature has been truly too great to
be easily overcome. This authority became truly
formidable when it was enforced by the power of
a long united empire and supported by a fairly

extensive system of education, the sole object of which has been to win official honour and recognition on the strength of the ability to read and write in the classical language.

Moreover, there was lacking in the history of spoken Chinese one important factor without which the authority of the classical language could never be destroyed. That important factor is a conscious and frank recognition of the fact that the classical language is a dead language and as such is disqualified to continue as the national language of a modern nation. Dante not only wrote in the vulgar tongue, but also defended it in his treatise *De vulgari eloquentia*. Boccaccio, too, was a conscious defender of the language he employed as literary medium. In France, the *Pléiade* were also conscious advocates of the French language; indeed, Du Bellay, one of the poets who formed the *Pléiade*, wrote *La défense et illustration de la langue française*, in which he asserted the right of the French language to stand as a medium of poetic expression. It is this element of conscious advocacy that was lacking in the case of spoken Chinese. There were large numbers of writers who were in one way or another attracted by the vulgar tongue and wrote in it. There were none, however, who openly questioned the supreme authority of the classical language or who consciously defended the living tongue as the only legitimate medium of literary composition. And it is this absence of an articulate movement which has made it possible for the dead language to reign supreme two thousand years after its death.

What the recent literary revolution did was to supply this very factor which was lacking in the long history of the living tongue, and to openly declare that the classical language has been long dead and that the *pei hua* which has been the literary medium for many centuries, is and will be the *only* proper and effective means of literary expression in verse as well as in prose. " No dead language can produce a living literature," was the war cry of the literary revolution. Its constructive policy is summed up in the motto, " Produce literature in the national language, and you shall have a national language of literary worth."* In 1916, the present writer made a resolution never to write any poetry except in the spoken language. The first public declaration of the revolution was published on the first day of the year 1917. The controversy went on for two years ; after that, opposition gradually died down. Since the summer of 1919, the *pei hua* has spread far and wide. In 1920, the Ministry of Education issued an order to the effect that, beginning with the fall opening of that year, the national language should be taught in the first two grades of the primary school. In the course of a few years, all the grades

* For the war literature of the literary revolution, see Hu Shih, *Selected Writings*, vol. I., pp. 1-320.

in the primary schools will be using the living tongue in the place of the classical. This change has of necessity affected the middle and normal schools where the primary teachers are trained, and these higher schools are anticipating the coming change by voluntarily adopting texts in the vulgate. Most of the recent publications have been in the vulgate. The newspapers and periodicals have in most cases ceased to publish poems in the classical language, and " new poems " in spoken Chinese are taking their places. It is safe to say that the controversial period is now almost over, and the era of constructive and creative work is before us.

The moral of this easy success of the literary revolution is obvious. It was not the work of any individual or individuals that has brought about its success. The time has long been ripe for this revolution ; two thousand years of collective effort in linguistic revision and ten centuries of literary activity in the living tongue—these are the real factors which have made such a rapid success possible. The common sense of our people has for twenty centuries been unconsciously but steadily and incessantly preparing for this day. The literary revolution of the last five years is no more than a culmination of twenty centuries' historical evolution. All unconscious processes of natural evolution are of necessity very slow and wasteful. Once these processes are made conscious and

5

articulate, intelligent control and experimentation become possible, the work of many centuries may be telescoped into a few years, and an easy success befall those who are in reality, to use a classical phrase, " getting the credit which properly belongs to Nature."

February, 1922.

IV

THE CONFUCIAN GOD-IDEA*

By Y. Y. Tsu

St. John's University, Shanghai

THE researches of Legge, De Groot, Ross, and others have made clear to us the main features of the ancient faith of China, as reflected in the old classical literature, especially in the Books of History and Poetry, the Shu-king and the Shih-king. De Groot's theory is that the core of Chinese religion, past as well as present, is animism. But other scholars, like Legge and Ross, do not share his view. It is true, they say, that spirits of the hills, rivers, and valleys and their worship are recorded in the Classics, but the first place in thought and in worship in ancient times was always given to *T'ien* or *Shangti* (Heaven or "Lord on High"). *T'ien* or *Shangti* was the supreme power or being in the universe, and all others, man or spirit, were subordinate to Him. And so they conclude that the ancient religion of China was monotheism. In the words of Legge, "five thousand years ago the Chinese were monotheists—not henotheists, but monotheists, and this monotheism was in danger of being corrupted, we

* Originally published in *Christian China.*

have seen, by a nature worship on the one hand, and by a system of superstitious divination on the other."*

Whether the ancient religion was pure monotheism or not, some kind of unity of religious thought had already been achieved, the existence of a supreme being or power ruling over kingdoms and men was acknowledged. But what was the supreme being or power whose existence men acknowledged ? Was it impersonal or personal, a moral principle or a righteous God ? Legge thinks that *T'ien* or *Shangti* is equivalent to the Christian term, God, or, at least, the Jewish term, Jahve. He says, " *T'ien* has had much of the force of the name Jahve, as explained by God Himself to Moses ; *Ti* (*Shangti*) has presented that absolute deity in the relation to men of their lord and governor. *Ti* was to the Chinese fathers, I believe, exactly what God was to our fathers, whenever they took the great name on their lips."† If the interpretation is correct, then we may rejoice with Soothill " that great preparation has been made in China for Christian enlightenment in the recognition of a Power above, great, beneficent, and just, who rewards virtue and punishes vice, and who can be approached in prayer."‡

A somewhat different attitude is taken by Suzuki in his *History of Chinese Philosophy*. He says, " It may not be altogether proper to consider Shang Ti

* Legge, *Religions of China*, 1880, p. 16.
† *Ibid*, p. 10.
‡ Soothill, *Three Religions of China*, 1913, p. 144.

as a being residing in heaven (t'ien). Though it is certain that he was not merely a moral power nor the personification of Heaven as some Christian missionary scholars of Chinese religion are inclined to believe, he was not a person in the fullest sense of the word. But he had something of personality in him and could properly be called " he " instead of " it." There is no doubt, however, that the early Chinese did not conceive their Shang Ti as did the Jews their Yahveh. When the Chinese spoke of Shang Ti, they had in their minds something of an august, supreme being in Heaven above, who was the arbiter of human destiny, though not their creator. He did not, exactly speaking, reside in Heaven, but Heaven was his material or objective expression. Figuratively speaking, Heaven was Shang Ti, and Shang Ti was Heaven."*

In other words, we have certain terms and expressions, which have been handed down from the remote past, and which are current more or less at the present time, but their exact meaning, as far as the ancients were concerned, is a matter of uncertainty, depending upon our ways of interpretation. In trying to interpret passages in the ancient classics, we have to bear in mind the following points : First, our personal beliefs are apt to colour our interpretation. There is always a great temptation for us to read into the passages the meaning that

* Suzuki, *History of Chinese Philosophy*, 1914, p. 174.

is most congenial to us. In religious matters, because of our great interest, this temptation is especially strong. We are inclined to idealise the ancient religion of China, in our effort to discover the so-called "preparation" in China for the Christian religion.

Secondly, in dealing with the religious ideas of the ancient Classics, we must remember that we are dealing with a state religion, the religion of the imperial court, and not the religion of the common people. The Court, for reasons of its own, might uphold an exalted monotheism, while the people might all the time, as De Groot contends, be sunk in the grossest animism.

Thirdly, literary expressions should not be received without critical estimation of their real value as distinguished from their face value. The ideals we proclaim in public are as a rule higher than those we live by in private. We are used to certain high-sounding ethical statements in governmental proclamations and professions and we know they are merely formal and conventional expressions, with little reality behind them. Similarly, we should accept the lofty religious expressions in the Classics with reserve. They might be merely a part of the impressive paraphernalia of state rule, based upon the Divine Right theory. In this connection we recall Legge's attempt to prove the exalted faith of the nation by the language of the hymns and prayers used by the Ming emperors at the Worship of Heaven.* Those hymns and prayers were wonderful, breathing the spirituality of the psalms of David and Solomon, but could we be sure that they were more than beautiful poetic forms composed for specific occasions and read, perhaps, by the emperors, with no more comprehension than a child has when reciting the " Great Learning," or the Analects of Confucius ?

Finally, the best interpretation is that afforded by historical development. By the fruits we shall know of the nature of the tree. To appreciate the quality of the ancient religion, we should not only study the literary remains of the past, but also examine the religious conceptions of the living who trace their spiritual ancestry to the ancient source. We should therefore find out the religious conceptions of the Confucianist scholar of to-day. He may gave been influenced in his thinking by Buddhist and Taoist doctrines, and in recent years by Western sciences and philosophies, but in the main he is the faithful product of that culture, recorded in the Classics, standardised by Confucius and his followers, and broadly known as Confucianism.

Let us proceed in our discussion in the following order: 1. The ancient faith. 2. The religious ideas of Confucius. 3. The religious ideas of Chutze, the foremost expositor of Confucianism, A.D. 1130-1201. 4. The religious ideas of the present-day scholars.

* Legge, *The Notions of the Chinese Concerning God and Spirits*, 1852, p. 23ff.

1. *The ancient faith.* The ideas about God, that is about *Shangti* or *T'ien,* in the Books of History and Poetry, are summarised by Soothill as follows : " He hears and sees ; He enjoys offerings ; He has a heart, or mind ; He is aided by men, and deputes His work, especially to kings and their ministers ; He can be honoured and served ; He is awe-inspiring, of dread majesty, and to be feared ; He confers on men their moral sense, and makes retention of this favour dependent on moral character ; His will is glorious, may be known, and must be complied with ; a virtuous king is after His own heart, but He will have no regard to the ill-doer ; with such a one He is angry ; the virtuous king He will reward with ease and dignity ; the appointment to kingly office is in His hands, such appointment is contingent, and favour may be lost ; He protects, but may withdraw His protection ; He warns, corrects, and punishes the evil king, even afflicts, ruins, and destroys him, and of this instances are clearly given."

" T'ien gives birth to the people ; It gives valour and wisdom to princes ; It gives blessings to the good and woes to the evil ; It ordains the social order the religious and social ceremonies, and human virtues ; It sends down rain ; It is gracious to men and helps them ; Its will is unerring ; It does not shorten men's lives, they do that themselves ; It is not bound to individuals by ties of biased human affections ; It commands men to rectify their character ; It gives man his nature, compassionates him, and grants his desires ; It is only moved by virtue, but men may cry and weep and pray to It, for It will hear."*

In discussing the Chinese ideas about God, Suzuki points out the interesting fact that He was never conceived of as having close personal relationship with human beings, or as having manifested Himself to them in any direct way through the senses. " He was a quiet, deliberate, ethical power that discharged or exercised his function rather impassively. He never showed himself in the midst of fires, thunders, or lightnings to vent his personal ire upon the creatures below. The Chinese never caught a glimpse of their God. He was hidden far up in the azure skies, he could not be brought into immediate personal touch with mortals."† God was conceived of pre-eminently as the moral authority of the universe, and in this aspect He was supreme and His will absolute. His dealings with men had to do primarily with moral conduct. A morally good life was the only way to get His favour. In other words, the strongly practical Chinese mind did not waste itself in vain imagination but made full use of its religion in promoting the welfare of common-day life. And so, while weak in spiritual

* Soothill, p. 143-4.
† Suzuki, p. 129.

fervour, the ancient faith was strong in ethical application. This characteristic, rather than decreasing as time went on, increased to such proportions that finally ethics overshadowed religion, and spiritual interests were lost sight of through concentration of attention to mundane affairs.

2. *The religious ideas of Confucius.* Confucius was pre-eminently a moralist. His interests were this-worldly. He had no taste for metaphysical speculation or religious contemplation. Excepting the one reference to his desire for the study of the mysteries of the Book of Changes, he consistently devoted himself to the study and solution of the practical problems of human relationships, and the teaching of right conduct. He showed no curiosity for the mysterious and unknown, and discouraged his disciples in their efforts to understand those things. His own words are well-known.*

" Not knowing how to serve men, how could we
    serve spirits ? "

" Honour the gods, but leave them alone."

" How could we know about death, when we
    have not understood life ? "

" Sacrifice to the spirits, as if they were here."

" Having offended Heaven, it is vain to pray for
    forgiveness."

" If I say the dead have consciousness, I am afraid
    the filial sons will neglect the living and serve

* Confucius' Sayings in Chinese.

the dead ; but if I say the dead have no consciousness, I am afraid the unfilial sons will give up burying their dead and sacrificing to them. Whether the dead have consciousness or not, we shall know it when we ourselves die. It is not too late."

These utterances, given in reply to the questions of the disciples concerning the occult, mysterious death, ghosts, and the spiritual world, reveal to us the attitude of the Sage, in the public rôle of the Teacher. In his private life, he showed strong faith in the Providence of Heaven as giving him his allotted life and work on earth, and protecting him against the evil designs of his enemies. On two occasions, he used the highly religious words, " Heaven has entrusted me with a mission, what can my enemies do to my life ? "* Furthermore, sometimes in his quiet hours, he did allow questionings about the " other world " to trouble his mind. " How surpassing great are the powers of the spirits. Looking, we cannot see them ; listening, we cannot hear them ; embodying themselves in things, they cannot be neglected. They make all men bathe, fast, put on sacrificial apparel and worship them. Vague and yet pervading, they seem to be above and around us."* But whatever his private religious views, Confucius in his public life as Teacher was an agnostic and positivist.

* Confucius' Sayings in Chinese.

In those days there were other schools of thought than that represented by Confucius. For example, Laotze and his followers were building up a philosophy, mystical, spiritual, and idealistic, defiantly antagonistic to the utilitarian and materialistic system of Confucius. Then there was Muh-tze, whose essays on Universal Love, the Existence of God and His attributes contain many conceptions which are strikingly similar to Christian teaching.* But through his strong personality, his conservatism, and his assumption of the rôle of the champion of ancient culture, Confucius was able to win Chinese thought to his standard and to make his school the orthodox, and the rival schools heretical. Henceforth Confucianism reigned supreme. As far as the religious development of the nation was concerned, this victory of Confucianism was a decided set-back, for the spirit of Confucianism, after its Founder, was sceptical and unfavourable to religious growth. Although it professed to preserve the ancient culture, and inherited the Classics as sacred literature, Confucianism contributed nothing to the enrichment of religious thought, the germs of which were embedded in that literature. The God-idea of the Classics instead of being clarified, grew dim and vague in the atmosphere of Confucianism, and finally, in the ambiguous term, T'ien, it became no more than

* Muh-tze's essays " Universal Love," " Against War," " Will of Heaven," " Knowledge of Spiritual Beings," etc.

an impersonal moral principle or law of the universe.

3. *The religious ideas of Chutze.* Chutze was the greatest expositor of Confucianism and commentator of the Classics. He lived in the Sung Dynasty, known as the Period of Confucian Renaissance, and was the chief exponent of the so-called " modern Confucianism " which has come down to our day. The illustrious Emperor K'ang-hsi, admiring Chutze as the true teacher of Confucian orthodoxy, appointed a commission of fifteen learned scholars to collect and publish all his known works. The result was the *Complete Works of Chutze*, in sixty-six volumes. It is unnecessary to reproduce all that Chutze said on religious matters. They are found especially in Volumes XLIX. and LI.

In his cosmogony, there was no place for a Creator. *Li* and *Chi* or Law and Air, or, in the language of Physics, Matter and Force, were the eternal dualism sufficient to explain the universe and all things therein, including life and mind.* The universe was, to borrow Spencer's phrase, a moving equilibrium, and subject to successive evolution and dissolution. This theory of evolution and dissolution is almost Spencerian, but Chutze gave as reason for the universe returning to chaos or dissolution the climax of human wickedness. He

---

* Quotations from Chutze regarding Creation.

did not commit himself to any position affirmative or negative, in regard to the existence of God. But once, when asked point-blank whether the Classics meant an actual Supreme Being in Heaven, in such sentences as " *Shangti* sends down the virtuous nature upon the people," " Heaven protects the people and appoints princes," " Heaven generates things, and increases their powers according to their capacity ; upon the good it sends down innumerable felicities, and on the evil innumerable calamities," etc., or merely employed the expressions as figures of speech to mean that owing to Law things were so, Chutze had to answer one way or the other, and his answer was, " Such statements have but one interpretation : it is merely that Law is so. The revolving Air from the beginning, has experienced fullness after decline and decline after fullness, ever thus revolving in a circle." Chutze's theory of the creation and fate of the universe is the typical Confucian theory of to-day. In its idea of successive worlds, of repeated creation and chaos, it reflects Buddhist influence, but the theory of dual forces, the positive and negative, was derived from the Book of Changes.

In regard to the existence of spirits, Chutze took the thoroughly orthodox attitude. " Those that have neither form nor shade are difficult to apprehend. Do not bother about them. Devote yourself to the work of daily existence which calls for continual exertion. The Master has said, " Not knowing how to serve men, how could we serve spirits ? " " How could we know about death, when we have not understood life ? " " He has said all there is to say about the matter." " Whether there are spiritual beings or not, it is not easy to tell in an off-hand way. Even if I told you, would you understand and believe ? You should try to understand first the natural law ; then this question will be cleared by itself. Someone asked the Master about them He replied, ' Honour the spirits, but leave them alone.' This is wisdom. Let us try to understand what ought to be understood, but leave what we cannot understand aside for the present. When you have understood perfectly the principles of daily life, you will naturally perceive the law about spiritual beings."*

But Chutze did try to explain in a materialistic way the existence of spirits, especially ancestral spirits, as the Worship of Ancestors called for.† At death, the breath leaves the body and is scattered and mingled with the universal air. But it is capable of coming together again at the time of ancestral worship, on the law that the like responds to the like. That is, the descendants who conduct the worship have the same breath in them that once animated their ancestors. When the descendants in sincerity and concentration of spirit beckon the

* Chutze on Spirits. Vol. LI.
† Chutze on ancestral worship. Vol. I.

ancestral spirit to return to the house, on such occasions the scattered spirit as capable of assembling again and returning. However, this " re-formation " of the scattered spirit into a unity is only temporary, being held together only by the intense concentration of the worshipper's mind during the worship. And so it is impossible for the ancestral spirit to unite and reincarnate itself in a body and thus have a second life, such as the Buddhists teach. Thus Chutze tried to explain ancestor worship. His explanation undoubtedly is the one accepted and current to-day.

4. *The religious ideas of the present-day Confucianists.* In order to ascertain the religious ideas of the present-day Confucianists, we recently put the question, " What does *T'ien* or *Shangti* mean according to the Confucian standard ? " to a number of Chinese scholars. The following replies are given because we believe they are typical of the present attitude of the educated people of the country outside of the Christian Church.

One scholar, a man of both Chinese and Western learning, and editor of an important educational magazine, says : " *T'ien* or *Shangti* in Chinese means exactly the same as God in English. But the God-idea is now discredited by the educated people. We do not believe in a personal God any more."

This man has spoken for a very large number of people. In matters of religion they have done no independent and deep thinking for themselves. Their Confucian education has pre-disposed them to agnosticism and unbelief. They accept certain views of well-known men, like Huxley and Spencer, as their own and consider the questions therein involved thus closed and settled. They have thrown overboard the idea of a personal God as being incompatible with the teachings of modern science. These people consider all religions as superstition and so cannot see any good in the Christian religion. We are inclined to entertain the hope that Christianity by its higher conception of God, may resuscitate and purify the Chinese idea of God and so lead men back to Him. But very often the effect of the contact of Christianity with the native religion is to produce conflict, and in their defiance of Christianity the native scholars would even throw away their old faith in God.

Another scholar, an educationalist widely known among Chinese and missionary educational circles, made this reply, " Let us exclude for the present the beliefs of the ignorant classes and consider the religious attitude of the educated classes only. To us, the *T'ien* or *Shangti* is a collective [noun ?] and stands for all that is mysterious and unexplained. The ancients were surrounded by mysteries and they had no means of understanding them and so invented the belief in the existence of a mysterious being which they called *T'ien* or *Shangti*. The idea has persisted to this day because it has been found a useful means of social control. The ignorant classes have no self-control. The 'personal God' idea excites fear and so acts as restraint upon their conduct. As to the references in the Classics about the justice of Heaven, of rewards and punishments, that is only a way of writing or speaking. There is in Nature the law of cause and effect, which works positively, and so there is no necessity for postulating a Personal Being in the universe dispensing rewards and punishments."

That religion is useful as a police force in dealing with the ignorant classes that are weak in self-control is an idea that one meets with all the time. The idea is generally entertained by the educated classes with a good deal of self-complacency, for the other side of the statement is that the educated person who knows his duties and rights has no need for religion. To them religion is something that will be outlived. When science gets at the mysteries that still remain and throws on them the light of knowledge, then religion will disappear.

A third scholar, who is a professor of Chinese History and Philosophy in a university, made this reply, " I have thought a great deal on the subject. It seems to me, Christians and Confucianists do not differ very much in the belief in the existence of Shen Ling (spiritual and divine beings), but in one thing we differ fundamentally. Christians say, 'We know that God is personal,' whereas we Confucianists say, ' We do not know, for we have no way of finding out what God is like.' "

This agnosticism is characteristic. God exists but He remains the Unknowable. This is the Creed of Confucianism. The first part makes you glow with pleasant anticipation of the wonderful vistas of spiritual insight that may be opened to you, but the second part slams the door right to and you are face to face with a solid stone wall. This stone wall of agnosticism is more difficult to surmount than open hostility, because the agnostic is always self-satisfied. Doubt is the prerequisite of inquiry and knowledge, but the agnostic excludes doubt, for he is positive of his own ignorance. He says human intellect is finite ; it is vain for it to strive to know the Unknowable. " Honour the gods, but let them alone."

As another example of the religious attitude of the modern Confucianist—this time, a written testimony—we quote from the *New Citizen Magazine* edited by Liang Chi-chao, the foremost living scholar of China, and published about ten years ago. " The religions of the world may not be identical in their aims, but they are alike in urging respect of Heaven and love of man. But while Jesus said, ' I am the Son of God,' Mahomet, ' I am God's Prophet,' Buddha, ' In heaven above and on earth below, I am alone Great,' Confucius said only this, ' I am trying to follow and support the development of Heaven and Earth.' But really Confucius' aim is the soundest of all, for the edification of mankind, and cannot be likened to the empty claims of the other religious leaders. . . . All religions talk about heaven and hell, but Confucius silenced all curiosity about spirits and the spiritual world by saying, 'Not knowing how to serve men, how could we serve spirits ? ' . . . The ancients were stupid ; without a heaven it was impossible to encourage them in good work, and without a hell it was impossible to restrain them in evil doing. Later knowledge became fuller and civilisation more advanced. Everyone knew that he must do his duty while he had a breath in him, and he dared not and cared not to stop one moment and waste his time in inquiring about heaven above or in contemplating with fear the hell underneath. He knew that if everyone did his best to fulfil the law of human life, it was the true way of what Confucius called 'following Heaven and Earth.' When the world reaches this stage, the religion of humanity will prevail. In short, do not indulge in empty talk about the mysterious and hidden, but converse about the common-day food and drink facts of existence, and the teachings of Confucius will have become triumphant."*

In conclusion, we may say that Confucianism has very little to tell us about God. The most

* *The New Citizen Magazine.*

generally used word for the God-idea is *T'ien*. It is ambiguous and stands for a personal Being at one time and an impersonal object at another, and no attempt has been made to define its nature. " Heaven has five titles : In our great respect for it, it is called, Heavenly Emperor ; to show its extent, it is called Great Heaven ; on account of its benevolence, it is called Merciful Heaven ; as it is above us and looks down at us, it is called High Heaven ; it is azure, as we look at it from afar, and so it is called, Azure Heaven."* Since Chutze and the Sung Dynasty, *T'ien* has lost its personal quality, and is identified with Natural Law or just Nature. " There is only one nature and no other. Referring to its substance, it is called heaven ; considered as ruler or lord, it is called *Shangti* (God) ; viewed as functioning, it is called fate ; as given to men, it is called disposition ; as controlling the body, it is called mind."† Such expressions as the " Virtue of Heaven " (*T'ien Tuh*), the " Reason of Heaven " (*T'ien Li*) and the " Word of Heaven " (*T'ien Tao*) are commonly used in literature of the present-day, but they are only figurative and poetic names for Nature and Natural Law. In short, to the Confucianists, the question of God and man's personal relationship to Him is a dead issue, for they are not interested in religion.

* Five Titles for Heaven.

† Wang Yang Ming (A.D. 1472-1529), the greatest scholar of Ming Dynasty. See *Philosophy of Wang Yang Ming*, Heiuke, 1916.

V

PRESENT TENDENCIES IN CHINESE BUDDHISM*

By Y. Y. Tsu

St. John's University, Shanghai

IN the rapid transformation of thought and life which is sweeping over Eastern Asia as a result of the impact of Western civilisation upon Oriental culture, there is one phase that is being watched with special interest by students of the history of religions on account of what it portends for the spiritual future of the Oriental peoples in particular and of the world in general, namely, the reaction of the old religions to modern influences. The disruptive effect of modern science upon ancient faiths is well known, but it is not to be supposed that the latter are so valueless and discredited as to succumb readily to the onslaught of new ideas and pass out of existence quietly without an effort at self-defence. On the contrary, the danger that faces them serves often as a powerful stimulus to rouse the old religions to renewed activity and reformation in an attempt to adapt themselves to changed conditions and so

* Originally published in the *Journal of Religion*.

retain their hold upon the loyalty of their followers. A classic instance of this kind in European religious history is the so-called Counter-Reformation within the Roman church and the accelerated development of its missionary zeal immediately following the Protestant Reformation. We find to-day in India reform movements within Hinduism, as indicated by the organisation of the Brahma Samaj and similar bodies; in Japan, the nationalisation of Shinto and the active revival of Buddhism; and in China the frustrated attempt to make Confucianism the state religion of the republic and lately signs of awakening in Chinese Buddhism after centuries of quiescent existence.

It will be recalled that in the history of Buddhism, China occupies a very important place. It was here that reformed or Mahayana Buddhism received its greatest development and from here spread into Korea and Japan. In the sixth century, when Buddhism was threatened with extinction in the land of its birth, Bodhidharma, the twenty-eighth Indian Patriarch, removed his seat from India to China and became the first Chinese Patriarch, thus making China the centre of the Buddhist church of that time. Modern students of Buddhism know that for much of our knowledge of the life and teachings of Sakyamuni and of the history of India and its condition in the time of the founder, we are indebted to the records of the Chinese Pilgrims,

Fah-hsein, Hiuen-tsang, and I-ching, who visited India in the fourth and seventh centuries and spent years of research there. Only through the French translation of Renusault in 1837 did any of these records become first available for Western scholars, and it is interesting to note in passing that the exact birthplace of Buddha was not located until toward the end of the nineteenth century, with the help of data found in those records. While it is correct to say, as Fenollosa and others have done, that China owes much of its finest in literature and art to Buddhism, it is equally correct to say that Buddhism in its historic development and expansion owes much to China. China is still the largest Buddhist country in the world, and in its language the most complete and extensive canon of Mahayana Buddhism is to be found. What will become of Buddhism in China will largely determine the fate of that religion in Asia, and on this account the present manifestation of new life-currents running through this old faith in China is of unusual interest and significance.

The reform movement in Chinese Buddhism began a little over ten years ago in the closing decade of the now defunct Manchu Dynasty. Those were thrilling days for the nation, astir in its every part with new life. Within the compass of those ten short years were crowded together events of tremendous moment, such as had never occurred at any

other time in the history of Eastern Asia. The year
1898 saw the abortive launching of the educational
and political reforms by Emperor Kuanghsu in
collaboration with K'ang Yu-wei, which brought
down upon them the fury of the then reactionary
Empress Dowager and resulted in the virtual
imprisonment of the Emperor and the flight of
K'ang from the country. Two years later, in 1900,
came the cataclysm of the Boxer Uprising, the
humiliation of the Imperial Court and its ignominious
flight to far-away Sian-fu. When the Empress
Dowager returned to Peking she was a wiser woman,
and espoused the cause of reform. In 1904-5 the
war between Japan and Russia was fought and the
spectacular victory of Japan over the forces of the
northern Octopus stirred the hearts of all Asiatic
peoples with new hopes and ambitious dreams of
the future. In 1908 the Imperial Court, after
having sent special commissions to Japan and Europe
for the study of constitutional government, and
having received their favourable report, announced
a programme for the gradual transformation of the
government into a constitutional monarchy and
authorised self-government for the provinces and
districts. Had the programme been worked out to
its culmination, China would have been a constitutional monarchy in 1913. But something happened
which deflected the course of events. In 1908
occurred the mysterious death of Emperor Kuanghsu,

still in his thirties, simultaneously with that of the Empress Dowager ; with the strong hand of the old lady withdrawn from the helm, the ship of state drifted into a condition which set the stage for the Revolution of 1911.

It was in those days of national self-consciousness and social and political upheaval, which wrought havoc to conventional attitudes and antiquated traditions, that the Buddhist church first felt the shock of changed times and the challenge of the new day. For better self-preservation and expression the Chung Hua Fu Chiao Tsung Hui (Chinese National Buddhist Society) was organised under the leadership of Chi Ch'an Ho Shang, abbot of Tien T'ung Ssu Monastery, Ningpo. The inauguration meeting was held at Liu Yun Ssu Monastery, Shanghai, in April, 1910, and an ambitious programme was adopted, of which the following were its chief provisions (free translation) :

1. This society is formed by the union of all Buddhist monks.

2. With branches all over the country, it exercises supervision over all the monasteries and monks.

3. All monks, formally admitted into the Order, are given certificates attesting to their membership in the society.

4. No monk is permitted to receive any pupil [candidate for the Order] unless the candidate is a bona-fide applicant and of good family.

5. No monastery is permitted to alienate any of its property without authorisation from the society.

6. Observance of monastic rules should be strictly enforced ; for violation of the same rules, monks are to be punished.

7. Seminaries for the training of candidates for the Order are to be established, and in it Buddhist scriptures and Chinese classics are to be taught.

8. Persons under twenty years of age are not to be admitted into the Order ; also those who have not had three years of theological training.

9. For monks to hire themselves out for the performance of funeral services, especially appearing in funeral processions, is considered derogatory to the dignity of the monastic order, and so the practice is to be strictly prohibited.

We note that the society aimed to purify the monastic order of its existing evils.   Of them, the two most prominent are the ignorance of the monks in the elements of their own religion and the mercenary spirit of the monks in rendering their religious services to the people ; hence the emphasis placed upon better theological preparation of the candidates and the prohibition of the monks taking part in the funeral services.

Other societies that appeared at that time in different parts of the country were : Fo Chiao Kung Hui (the Buddhist Church Club), Chung Hua Wang Man Tsu Hui (the Yellow Swastika Society, corresponding to the Red Cross Society in its objects), Fo Chiao Chin Te Hui (Buddhist Moral Endeavour Society), Fo Hsueh Yen Kyeu She (Buddhist Research Society), etc. Two magazines were published as organs of the new movement : *Fo Chiao Ts'ung Pao* (Buddhist Miscellany) and *Fo Chiao Yeuh Pao* (Buddhist Monthly).

This was the first wave of Buddhist revival. In its nature it was political rather than spiritual, and it resulted in better organisation rather than moral reformation. As a reaction to external circumstances enthusiasm surged high at first, but there was nothing within the Order to uphold it, and so, when the first impetus had spent itself, the movement fell to pieces. One by one the activities such as educational and charitable institutions, lectures and magazines were given up, and the various societies, which had sprung up like mushrooms, disappeared as quickly.

In justice to the movement it must be said that the Revolution of 1911, which resulted in the formation of the Republic, was at least in part responsible for the breakdown of the revival. The spirit of the Revolution was iconoclastic, especially toward monastic Buddhism, and the Republican Government has not dealt kindly with it. Although the constitution has promised religious liberty and equality of treatment of all religions, yet the government has seen fit to exercise stringent supervision over Buddhism. In doing this it is merely keeping up the tradition of the past dynasties, which had always looked upon Buddhism as a ward of the State, owing to the fact that historically Buddhism was introduced into China through royal patronage and had been more or less dependent for its support upon the munificence of the imperial court. Perhaps the other reason for government supervision is that official China, being Confucianist in its political and social philosophy, is always apprehensive of a religion which values monastic life as superior to the life of the household, and so thinks that it should be carefully guarded against too successful a propagation lest it weaken the State, which is built according to Confucian tenets upon the family as its cornerstone.

Whatever the motive behind the governmental policy, soon after the political reorganisation of the country was fairly well in hand, President Yuan Shi-kai, first president of the Republic, ordered to be promulgated through Parliament in 1915, "Regulations for Government Supervision of Temples and Monasteries." While these regulations were supposed to apply to Buddhist and Taoist institutions without discrimination, it was clear that owing to the fact that Buddhist institutions far outnumber those of the Taoist faith and that Taoism has no monks anyway, the regulations would fall more heavily upon the Buddhists—in fact, that was the intention of the government. The government justified itself by arguing that temples and monasteries are public institutions and many of them are of historic and artistic importance, and so supervision was necessary to prevent their falling into private hands. The chief features of the regulations are : (1) registration of temples and monasteries, monks and nuns ; (2) taxation of temple property ; (3) non-alienation of temple property ; (4) subjection of religious activities and preaching services to police regulation.

This action brought forth vehement protest from the Buddhists, and because of this protest and also of the fall of the Yuan régime in 1916, the regulations were not enforced. But in retaliation for the protest, the government closed down the National Buddhist Society on the pretext that its existence was dangerous to public safety. The society was reorganised after Yuan's fall, but in 1917 it was again closed by the government at the time when the regulations were put into effect.

As an illustration of the way the government has dealt with Buddhist establishments, when pressed by circumstances, we recall the fate of Lung Hua Ssu, an ancient and famous monastery in the western suburb of the city of Shanghai. In pre-republican days, it enjoyed wide popularity, not only on account of its architecture, but also because of its beautiful rural surroundings. In the springtime its courtyards were thronged with pilgrims and children who came to worship and enjoy the many-coloured peach blossoms for which the countryside around the temple is famous. Then came the Revolution of 1911 and with it the battalions of new soldiers in khaki uniforms. Some of them were despatched to Shanghai for its protection. But there were no barracks and the government had no money to build them. Someone with a business mind, but little capacity for spiritual values, suggested that the commodious equipment of Lung Hua Ssu was available, and the army could have it for less than a song, for the monks were powerless to resist. And so one morning, soldiers came, turned out the monks, and established themselves there. That was eight years ago and the khaki-uniformed soldiers are still there. The droning voices of the bonzes in their chanting, the temple bells, and the footsteps of pilgrims in springtime have all disappeared, and in their place one hears the mingled notes of the bugle and the drum, and the measured thud of the soldiers' boots resounding in the yards as they practice the goose-step to the rhythm of the " Left-Right " of the leader. A sight which one can hardly forget on entering the main hall is to see in place of the beautiful tapestries, candlesticks, kneeling stools, and burning lamps—the paraphernalia of worship and adoration—the entire floor space crowded with stacks of rifles with shining bayonets,

For effective propaganda the society publishes a monthly magazine, called *Hai Chao Yin* (the Voice of the Sea Waves). It aims to lift the voice of Mahayana Buddhism for the guidance of mankind tossed as it is by the waves of modern thought. The magazine contains (1) exposition of Buddhist doctrines, as, for instance, a new commentary of " Mahayana Craddhotpada-castra " (Awakening of Faith) ; (2) apologetics or defence of the faith in face of modern criticism ; (3) advocacy of reformation, as reorganisation of the monastic order ; (4) testimonials : stories of conversion experience, lives of saintly devotees, etc. ; (5) critical review of works on religion and philosophy, especially on Buddhism. It is of high literary quality and is edited by T'ai Shu Fa Sz himself.

About the early life of the new leader little is known. He is much sought after for spiritual advice and for conducting lecture and devotional meetings. His writings are read extensively and through them he exercises great influence upon thinking men and women of the day. He has travelled in Japan and there met some of the leaders of Japanese Buddhism. From his autobiographical sketch, which appeared in the first issue of the *Hai Chao Yin*, the following is extracted, as showing the spirit of the man :—

" T'ai Shu in youth did not know Buddhism. Later I was attracted to it and I studied deeply into

Buddhist books.   After some time knowledge of the Buddha came to me like a pearl, lost and found again, and with it, as with a mirror, I was enabled to see clearly through the changes of this life and the world.

"Toward the last days of the Tsing (Manchu) Dynasty, the wish gradually formed within me of applying the law of Buddha for the harmonising of the philosophies of ancient and modern times and of the east and the west, and of leading the nations of the whole world to follow the teachings of Sakyamuni. Since then, during the past decade, through circumstances favourable and unfavourable, whether travelling abroad or staying at home, whether engaged in mundane affairs or retired in lonely hermitage, this wish has not for one moment been permitted to leave my mind.

"Then the European War broke out. Added to the rottenness of the inward life of man was the brutal struggle of the outward world. I was convinced of the magnitude of human calamity, which like a wagon-load of hay on fire could not be extinguished with a cupful of water.

"Since it was ordained that I should wait until the ripe time to carry out my wish, I decided to make use of the waiting to exercise my religion [contemplation], and so I 'shut myself' on Pontoo Island for three years.

" After that, I travelled in Japan and Taiwan, and wherever convenient I preached the doctrine. [He published afterward an account of his travels.]

" The next year, I was invited to visit the South Sea Islands [where there are colonies of prosperous Chinese emigrants]. I formed the idea of building a national monastery. My observation leads me to feel that the monastic institutions in our country have fallen away from ancient pure ideals and are corrupt beyond reform. If I could raise the fund from people abroad, I would build the national monastery [as model of renewed and purified monasticism]. If I should fail to attain my object I would reconcile myself to the life of a wondering mendicant and, leaning upon Buddha's mercy, thus travel to my life's end.

" When I was at Pontoo, some earnest devotees requested me to lecture on ' Wei-shi-lun " [Shastra Vidyamatrasiddhi]. I talked to them about my wish to reform monastic institutions and my plan to go south. They also saw the works I have written. They strongly advised against the southern trip at the time, as the European War was at its height, and it would be difficult to raise money there, but urged me to publish my works and to organise a society for the promotion of Buddhism in China as the first step of my larger plans. And so we organised the ' Bodhi Society ' in Shanghai. . . ."

[Here he mentioned plans for establishment of

Buddhist University, model monasteries for training preachers, encouraging philanthropies, etc., also raising fund for trip around the world in the interest of Buddhism.]

" Lately I have been living in Chin-Van Yuan Monastery, on the side of the Western Lake, Hangchow. Here I had desired to live quietly for the practice of contemplation, but the members of the Bodhi Society have asked me to edit a new magazine, called *Hao Chao Yin* [the Voice of Sea Waves] to meet the needs of the time. I have consented to do it for one year, as the work is congenial to my original wish, and so for this year, I have decided to lay aside other work and devote myself to editing the magazine. What of the future, a year hence none can foretell. But at the close of ten thousand years, the Tathagata will surely raise up men to establish the Law and spread it throughout the world of the living. I shall wait awhile.

" Dated 20th Day of 11th Moon of 2946th year after Buddha (1920)—*H.C.Y.*, Vol. I."

T'ai Shu, being a monk himself, is fully conscious of the weakness of the Buddhist church (1) in the lack of efficient organisation for the propagation of the religion, and (2) in the corruption of the monastic order, and so he has addressed himself to the task of reorganisation and reformation. He proposes to have a national system embracing preaching chapels and parishes in every city, a certain number of monasteries and charitable institutions in each province, and a national monastery and university in the capital city of the country. As a part of the national institution he would have a library containing an extensive collection of Buddhist literature and a museum for Buddhist art. Into the museum he would have all images moved, so that other buildings could be free of them. Belonging as he does to the Dhyana or Meditation School, founded by Bodhidharma in the sixth century, T'ai Shu is opposed to idolatry and tolerates it only as an accommodation to the weakness of the masses. As to the monks, he would encourage manual labour as an antidote to laziness and would encourage more time being spent in meditation and study for spiritual development. In his account of his travels in Japan and Taiwan he had a brief reference to his daily life to the effect that it has been his practice to spend at least three or four hours every day in meditation, and he has never allowed a day to pass without it, even the busiest day, during the past ten years. How far he will be able to carry out the reforms which he has conceived in his mind only time will show. Meanwhile he has been influential in winning many serious minded men and women to the pursuit of the religious (monastic) life.

In the spring of 1920, three men renounced the world and entered the Order together, adopting as their religious names, Great Mercy, Great Awakening and Great Valour. They were literati and had served the Republic in public life, but were converted through the preaching of T'ai Shu to become teachers of the Law of Buddha. On taking the step each person wrote out a statement giving his reasons for his action. On reading these statements, which appeared in the *Hai Chao Yin*, one realises what a strong appeal the simple gospel of Buddha still makes to the minds of men and women in the East, who, dissatisfied with existing conditions of life, are seeking a way of escape whereby they can rise above the turmoil and adversities of troublesome life, be free from the shackles of circumstances, and have peace of mind. In the practice of self-discipline, of strenuously controlling and suppressing one's insatiable desires—the root of all misery in the world, as Buddha taught twenty-five centuries ago —men feel they have found the way of salvation for themselves and for others, and having found it they become, like Buddha himself, fervent messengers in bringing the truth to others. The following, taken from one of the above-mentioned statements, expresses the spirit of the present movement in Buddhism :—

" The Law of Buddha is the most true, most excellent, most profound, and most universal way for all phenomenal and supra-phenomenal worlds— unexcelled and the only one—because it meets the sore need of the world, which is spiritual and of the heart. Let us consider the recent world-war as a case to the point. Did it not arise on account of the greed, ignorance, and madness of human egotism ? The greater the desire, the greater the seeking. Blind movement leading to blind steps, eagerness for struggle, eagerness for victory, false grappling, false possession—from such activity [deeds] on the part of many there has resulted the world calamity. To go forward with such a heart unchanged, the more one tries to restore order, the greater will be the chaos. And so to seek for true, universal, and permanent peace and happiness, the only way efficacious is for everyone to be willing in his heart to reduce desire, to be contented, to cease struggling, and relinquish one's hold. Hence my conviction that world-salvation requires the Law of Buddha. But this cannot be accomplished without my earnestly and speedily proclaiming the Law among men. To do this, the best way is for me to strengthen my will, study the doctrine, and thus prepare myself to give my personal testimony of faith. Hence the primary step on entering the Order. My now doing this, namely, leaving family, and society, and learning the Law of Buddha, is to prepare myself for the task of saving the world with the Law. It is not dissimilar to my previous action of leaving home and studying military art to prepare myself for the task of saving my own country. The difference is that previously my aim was the salvation of my country and people, while now my aim is the salvation of all living creatures.— *H.C.Y.*, Vol. I."

Not only are men renouncing the world and entering the monastic order, but educated women are doing it also. In *Hai Chao Yin* was published a remarkable letter written by a young woman to T'ai Shu for spiritual advice. Documents of this kind, recording as this does the inner spiritual life in non-Christian religions, are not common or easily accessible, and so we have given below the letter as a whole :—

"At present, Buddhism has deteriorated and reached the lowest ebb. The main reason is the corruption of monastic orders, male and female. The monks and nuns do not know how to save themselves, not to think of their saving others. Not one out of a hundred can keep the discipline and read the sutras. This is indeed most sad. So I think we cannot hope for improvement of the condition unless there come forward monks and nuns, of genuine motive for saving the world, with deep knowledge of the Law and respect for the Order, determined (1) to purify the monastic life, and (2) to propagate the religion. But how few are such choice spirits, like your reverend self, and others [mentioned by name]. If only more would take up the monastic vow! But some say that one may serve Buddha without laying aside family and social life. In my opinion, at the present time, to purify monastic life and propagate the religion, it is absolutely necessary to shave off the hair and enter the Order. I am therefore greatly surprised to read in one of the numbers of the Magazine that you, reverend Sir, wrote, 'The best way is to practice bodhi without forsaking the world [becoming a monk].'' Now, you, reverend Sir, are yourself a monk; why then advise others against becoming monks? There must be a reason. Will you instruct me?

" Formerly I was a student at a school, and was not inclined to believe in Buddhism. Later unconsciously my faith sprang up and then I became convinced that the Law of Buddha is the absolute and only true religion, unbounded and most lovable. So, at the age of nineteen, I made a vow before Buddha, that in this life I would never marry, but give my life to Him as a nun. I have kept this vow for four years, and many times I wanted to shave off my hair, but was prevented by my parents. I am sorry that I cannot be a nun early in life. I have three friends with the same mind. One is married, but she daily thinks of shaving off her hair and 'forsaking the world'; only she is prevented from doing so by her husband. But she is persuading him to become a monk, and I won't be surprised if they two should 'forsake the world' together before the end of the year. For a girl to be able to shave off her hair and be a nun is the most happy thing. Now-a-days some nuns complain that their lives are unhappy, while the lives of lay-folk are happy. I really cannot understand their way of thinking. The other two friends were both my school-mates. One is called 'Pure root'; she has no parents, but a brother—none to prevent her— and so she became a nun in the spring of last year. The other is only eighteen, and yet her determination to 'forsake the world' is unusually strong. This year her mother wanted to betroth her to some one, and so she decided to leave home secretly. I recommended her to a certain nunnery. Of us four, two have already realised their wish, leaving my cousin and myself outside the fold. I feel grieved and also envious of their good fortune.

"At first we thought that by becoming nuns we would escape from the world's misery and sorrow, enjoy peace, and work off by penance some of our sinfulness. Furthermore, by becoming nuns we sisters could live together and never be separated, which is supreme joy.

"But now, after reading *Hai Chao Yin*, we know that 'to forsake the world' is to benefit others, not ourselves. Having known this my will to be a nun has become stronger than ever. I wish that I could now and here shave off my hair. I have a few questions which I hope my Master in the Law will answer fully. I shall be most grateful. (1) How could one secure parents' and elders' consent. (2) Failing to secure the consent, could one be justified in secretly leaving home and entering the Order ? (3) How could one get rid of the emotion of love ? (4) Could one abandon one's husband and be a nun ? (5) Is it right to persuade one's wife, husband, or others to 'forsake the world' ? (6) Is it right to abandon one's children and become a nun ? (7) If I were a man I would have chosen you, Sir, as my Teacher, but being a woman that is not proper. Could you recommend to me a nunnery where I can go ?

" In my study of the sutras, I have unfortunately no one to teach me. I can only try my best to recite them, with or without true understanding. In case I come across passages I cannot understand, would you permit me to write you for help ?

" . . . Kindly reply through the magazine. . . .

[*Signed :* Purified Heart].

" P.S.—I am determined, whatever happens, to shave off my hair this year. After becoming a nun, I propose to reform and change the life of the nunnery with all my might. I hope to ask your advice in the future."—Quoted from *H.C.Y.*, Vol. V.

As yet this spiritual revival in Buddhism is confined to a small group of educated monks and lay brothers. The vast mass of Buddhist monks and nuns (estimated at 400,000 monks and 10,000 nuns) are untouched by it. These still continue their religious life in the conventional way, bow before the image of Buddha, repeat the sutras without understanding, and trust to the magic passport, *Namo Omito Fo* (*Namu Amida Butsu*)—" Praise to Amida Buddha "—for entry into " Western Paradise " after death. The reformers have a great task before them in purifying and energising the faith of this multitude. Will the revival succeed in transforming Buddhism to meet the changed conditions and demands of modern life, so that it will stand out in Asia as a rival to Christianity or Mohammedanism for centuries to come, or will the revival fail in its object and leave this ancient religion to the fate of ultimate extinction from internal corruption, and external disruption ? The question is not easy to answer, but one feels that the essentially pessimistic spirit of Buddhism and its conception of the worthlessness of life are fundamentally opposed to and incompatible with the buoyancy of the modern spirit and the modern conception of the worthfulness of life, and unless Buddhism is transformed to fit in with the new age as a religion it has no vital message, although as a philosophy of life its influence will persist in men's thinking. But Buddhism with its pessimistic spirit and outlook amputated will no longer be itself, but become something else, although the name may remain. Buddhist reformers are trying hard to find a way out of the dilemma, and the probable course they will take, as indeed they have already done, is to return to Sakyamuni's Ethics of the Middle path and make it their creed and message. But in doing this the Buddhist reformers will meet with a serious difficulty in the question, What is the goal of the ethical life in a system that denies human personality and social reality ? And so when one reviews the work of the reformers, so heroic and devoted in their effort to stem the tide of dis-integration and to build up the glory of their religion in a new age, one senses in them a feeling of loneliness, want of self-confidence, and the absence of genuine zest, because of the lack of an adequate goal. We recall the pathos of what T'ai Shu, the leading reformer, said, " If I should fail to attain my object, I would reconcile myself to the life of a wandering mendicant, and, leaning upon Buddha's mercy, travel thus to my life's end."

St. John's University,
    Shanghai.

VI

THE IMPRESSION OF CHRISTIANITY MADE UPON THE CHINESE PEOPLE THROUGH CONTACT WITH THE CHRISTIAN NATIONS OF THE WEST

THIS article is not written because we wish ourselves to criticise any particular policy pursued or work done in China by the countries of the West, but because as Chinese Christians we much desire to see Christianity widespread in our country. It is based upon candid study of the facts as to the relations between China and foreigners in the past, and upon the present psychology of the people, our purpose being to supply to fellow-Christians in Europe and America material for studying the situation. We also wish to avail ourselves of the opportunity afforded by the meeting here of the World's Student Christian Federation. We do not expect that those in power in the countries of the West will make immediate changes in their programmes or policies of work, but we trust that the Christian students and leaders of the world, learning that the Chinese people really have such conceptions of Christianity, may, because of their earnest desire for the spread of that faith, give publicity to this article, that the material here presented may lead their people more carefully to think out the applications of Christian faith. If this is accomplished, we shall not have written in vain.

Again, since the contents of the article concern the conceptions of the Chinese people in regard to certain policies pursued and work done by the countries of the West, why should we speak of the impressions of Christianity made upon the Chinese people, and why, particularly, should we call the countries of the West Christian countries? There are two reasons. First, missionaries in China in presenting the case of Christianity, frequently take the most advanced countries in the West as examples, and also admit that the civilisation of these countries has been built up largely by people who believe in Christianity. Although, therefore, it is a question whether the countries of the West have really practised the principles of Christianity, nevertheless in this article we have temporarily to think of them as Christian countries. Second, usually people judge by deeds and not by words. The countries of the West, it is certainly true, have advanced because of their faith in Christianity. But as most of the people of China have never been in the West to observe the actual conditions, no matter how much the missionaries may praise their countries, the Chinese people see no proofs of their words.

On the other hand, the policies pursued, and the work done by these countries in China are a part of the actual experience of the Chinese people, and therefore much attention is paid to them. Although those who have pursued these policies and done this work may not really be Christian people, yet, since the Chinese think of them as from Christian countries, their acts and policies are considered Christian, and leave in the Chinese mind a certain definite impression as to what Christianity is.

As we have briefly stated the reason for writing this article, we are now prepared to mention some of the facts referred to. It is now several hundred years since China came into contact with the countries of the West. It is neither possible nor necessary to mention all the happenings between China and these countries. What we shall speak of are their diplomatic and economic policies toward China, and the educational and missionary work of these countries in China.

First, diplomacy. In the diplomatic dealings which China has had with foreign countries during the last hundred years, she has always failed to achieve her ends, and always had the worst of the bargain. On the whole she has received much benefit from her contact with foreign countries, but only a few far-sighted individuals hold this point of view. The people in general only know things as they happen. These happenings they criticise, often blaming other countries for them.   Foreign governments have been always reaching out to extend their power, and it has been easy in many places to disregard justice. China's Opium War with England was immediately followed by treaties with different countries permitting trade and missionary work. These countries, seeing China's weakness, have often taken advantage of her. Happenings of very minor importance, and the loss of a few lives have been used as a pretext to compel China to give up hundreds of miles of territory, and to pay hundreds of thousands in indemnities. Sometimes all kinds of concessions have been demanded without cause, using such ideas as the necessity for " balance of power " and " spheres of influence " to justify such actions. In fact, most of China's diplomatic dealings with foreign countries, and the treaties made with them, have been put through when she was defeated. In other cases, the threat of compulsion, backed by military power, has wrested treaties from her. It is true that recent Conferences, like those in Versailles and Washington, have openly professed to uphold justice, so that China has been able to send delegates to represent the opinion of her people, hoping to find redress for the injustices done her in the past. But among the countries represented at these Conferences there have been few who wished to see justice done to China. Always in the end they have put the benefit of their own countries first, so might has won and justice has been defeated.

Second, Economic Policies. China has repeatedly failed in her diplomatic relations with foreign countries and has been the victim of their aggressive policies to such an extent that she has not been able properly to develop in national strength. In addition, through internal troubles, the living conditions of the people have become more difficult. Foreign nations have recently changed from their former military aggression to economic permeation and exploitation, which fastens much more subtle and dangerous hands upon the national life. During these years the finance of the Chinese Government, aside from the balance from the foreign controlled customs and salt revenues, has looked to foreign loans. Looking at the matter superficially, we may say that foreign countries have greatly benefited China, but this benefit, how shall we differentiate it from the quenching of thirst with poison ?

On the other hand, the principle of self-sacrifice for others is incompatible with the principles of economics as generally understood. It seems too much to expect that foreign countries should do other than seek their own benefit and disregard others ; but, the people cannot understand when the representatives of the Western nations on the one hand talk about righteousness, love, and friend-ship, while on the other hand their governments practise these oppressive policies. Look at the insistence upon the payment of the indemnities with limitation of the raising of import duties. This they think is only to suck the blood and the fat of the Chinese people for the sake of adding to the wealth of foreign countries.

Third, Educational Work. The earliest steps taken towards the reformation of the educational system of China were in connection with the old examination system. It is a well-known fact that the schools started by the Christian Church in various places helped to give the impetus needed to produce this change, and that the foreign missionaries have greatly assisted in creating the modern system of education in China. We can never forget this. They have raised large sums of money in their own countries, and have come here to start schools and train leaders for China. The graduates of these missionary schools have served in different professions, and many of them have won their place in popular regard. Moreover, these schools have paid special attention to the children of poor families and have tried their best to help them. Since missionary educators have done so much to benefit the Chinese people, in what way can they criticise them ? First of all, they say that the objective of these missionary schools was to preach the doctrines of Christianity. But religion and education are to them two different things. Since missionary schools have as their objective the preaching of Christianity, they naturally did not pay as much attention to education as educational institutions should. Not having much contact with other local schools, they did not know of the new orders issued by the government, and so oftentimes did not change their old-fashioned text-books for years. Owing to the fact that they did not pay much attention to the Chinese course of study, they failed to secure Chinese teachers of the right type. Most of the students at these schools failed to appreciate Chinese studies to such an extent that they could not tell the general outline of Chinese history and geography. As to their character most of the emphasis was laid on the side of obedience and faithfulness, thinking that the type of men thus produced would make suitable preachers. But initiative and independence were not emphasised. The pupils were often left without adequate knowledge of world movements, and of the great happenings in their own country, except for the meagre amount given them in their school text-books. These are the grounds on which popular criticism rests.

Again, the principal and teachers were sometimes autocratic, exercising absolute authority over the students. They said that this was to train the students in obedience; but in fact, it tended to make education servile. Also, without regard to whether the students had been Christian or not, they compelled them to study the Bible, and to go through morning and evening prayers, contrary to the principle of religious freedom. This easily evoked ill-feeling on the part of the people. Sometimes they remarked that the missionary schools filled the young people's minds with legendary stories and thus spoiled them. This criticism may be exaggerated, but it is true that the missionaries have mixed up the objectives of religion and education. As a result, they have failed in realising completely their aim, and have at the same time earned the criticism of being over-conservative in education.

Fourth, Missionary Work. The people of the Western nations have come to China to preach Christianity. Chinese, while admiring the evangelistic enthusiasm of Christians, cannot but observe certain points open to criticism. We need not go too much into detail, but will merely mention several more important matters. The churches of the nations of the West, not only pray for the victory of their own countries in war-time, but also directly or indirectly use the strength of the Church to aid in war. Is this not contrary to Jesus' ideal of peace ? Again, Jesus' programme of world reconstruction certainly seeks the abolition of social and national evils, the turning of darkness into light. But the churches of the Western nations, wishing to preserve their own positions, too often keep silent as to the faults of their governments instead of fighting them. Again, they are complacent in the face of evil social customs. Is this, they ask, the spirit of Christian reconstruction?

Again, the Christian truth is evolutionary; and adaptable to humanity's changing need. But the churches of the present age still hold to the old theology of their forefathers, and to the creed of ancient times. They are not willing to make changes in the constitution of their organisations. They not only do not take the lead in social reform, but are even willing to be left behind. Seeing society advance they themselves do not want to be renewed or make any improvement. How can such organisations show the greatness and the universality of Christian truth? Again, they clearly see that the Chinese people in general have quite different ideas of Christianity from formerly and that the Christian Chinese in particular have also advanced in enlightenment. But the churches, lagging behind, have failed to train the right kind of leadership to meet this situation. It might almost seem as though the foreign missionaries sometimes feared that if the Chinese preachers were more highly cultivated, they could not so easily use them before.

Again, they know very well that the standard of living in all places in China has risen many fold, while the salaries of the Chinese preachers have not been advanced accordingly. Although they have seen preachers resign and enter other lines of work because of inability longer to suffer family financial difficulties as well as hunger and cold, still they do no seem to care. If we compare their condition with that of the Chinese preachers, the difference is very great. How far are these things from that teaching of equality which is Christian ! In a word, Christianity as preached, how sublime, how profound ! but if we consider the activities of the Church and the attitude of many of the missionaries, how far removed from that preaching !

From the facts which have now been presented in this paper, we see that the countries of the West have benefited China through contacts political, economic, educational, and religious. Recently these countries have promoted the limitation of armaments, the returning of the indemnities, the formation of the Consortium, the sending of the Educational Commission to China, and the forma- tion of independent Chinese Churches. These are all indications of progress. Some of the facts mentioned in this paper may never have a chance to appear again. It might seem unnecessary to relate things already past, but the political aggression, economic oppression, educational conservatism, and religious unreality, of which we have spoken, all these we still find existing in some measure, a fact which leaves a very bad impression in the minds of the Chinese people, and one which cannot easily be erased. They may continue to feel that Western nations have inflicted upon China such indescribable losses, that she will be unable soon to recover herself and make the needed progress in various phases of her life. We need not discuss this further. But from the standpoint of Chinese Christians, suppose they are asked, Can all this above-mentioned aggression, oppression, conservatism, and unreality exist in a Christian country ? What can they answer ? They may say, China has many weak points, and should not blame others more than herself. But as to the countries of the West, since they are " Christian " and " advanced " they should feel more responsibility to act according to Christian truth. For, as Jesus says : " To whomsoever much is given, of him shall much be required ; and to whom they commit much, of him will they ask the more."

VII

THE CHINESE CHURCH

By C. Y. CHENG (CHENG CHING YI)

Chairman of the National Christian Conference, Shanghai, 1922

IT is obvious that it is impossible to deal, in any measure of adequacy, with such a vast subject as that of the Chinese Church in a brief article of only a few thousand words. The question is at once many-sided and complicated. In this paper we can only touch upon a few of the more pressing problems that are facing the Church of Christ in this land of ours, and that from a purely Chinese point of view.

In dealing with the subject we may appear to some to be unduly bold and frank in expressing our opinions and ideas. This does not mean that we have found the solution to all the problems ; it rather indicates that there is a sincere desire on the part of Chinese Christians to meet the situation and to seek for further light.

The missionary body is China's best friend, and is the best friend of the Chinese Church. In none of the remarks made in this article, which may seem rather critical, is there any reflection upon our missionary friends, who have done, and are doing, their best for the Chinese Church. We are, under God, very grateful to our Western friends who have come to our midst with the noble idea of bringing to us the Glad Tidings of Salvation. Everything in this paper is written in the truest spirit of appreciation and friendliness.

While there are many points of excellence in the enriched Christian experience of our friends of the West which we desire to share and imitate, the time is fast coming for the naturalisation of the Christian Church in order to secure a more speedy Christianisation of China. Christianity is beyond and above racial and national differences, and is capable of becoming indigenous in every land ; Christianity in China is therefore Chinese Christianity. The Gospel is universal and is applicable to all mankind, but at the same time its varying elements should be adjusted to the needs of the people of the time.

It is important, we think, to know the circumstances under which the Chinese Church is trying to realise itself and to bear its burdens. In the hope that we may understand the situation better and thus be able to pray for it more intelligently, let us state some of the problems that are facing the Church of Christ in China at the present time. These problems may be broadly divided into two groups, namely, those related to the missions, and those related to the Church. Let us begin with the former.

We are not far wrong when we say that Christianity has come to China with a great deal of European colouring. In bringing to the people of the Orient the Gospel of Salvation, the missionary has brought with him much of the thought, manners customs, methods, temperament, and atmosphere of the West, some of which do not seem to be quite suitable for the people of the East. No one is to be blamed for this state of things. It is unavoidable. But it has given occasion to the rise of many problems which are being felt more acutely as the Church begins to take up its responsibilities.

The Oriental Christian is beginning to view the Christian message through his own eyes, and to realise that Christ has come to China not to destroy but to fulfil all that is beautiful, good and true in the past. For instance, the question of ancestor commemoration has been a subject often discussed at missionary meetings and conferences. The general practice of the mission churches has always been the rejection of everything connected with this custom. This has been one of the greatest hindrances to many who would otherwise have joined the Church and become its members. Thoughtful Christians to-day are trying to show to their non-Christian friends that, while they reject all that is superstitious and idolatrous in this commemoration, yet they wish to uphold and enrich all that which is in keeping with the teaching of the Christian religion.

Christian memorial services are therefore held each year by Churches and Christians to celebrate, in a Christian way, the commemoration of the departed parents. This has not only removed a very real difficulty and much misunderstanding, but has also enriched and beautified the ancient custom which, in its original simplicity, was perfectly commendable.

Because of the dominant position held by the missionary in the church, the Mission looms very much larger than the church. Many of the 6000 Protestant churches that are in existence in China to-day must still be regarded as " Mission Churches," *i.e.*, churches supported and to some extent controlled by the Mission. Circumstances have led the modern mission to adopt the method of supporting almost every branch of religious, educational, and benevolent activities. The mission is therefore a huge concern with property in land and buildings the value of which amounts to many millions. Church buildings, schoolhouses, hospitals, etc., are realities of the modern mission. It is estimated that no less than twelve million dollars silver are being spent in China by the various missions annually, not counting money spent on property. One leading missionary once said that he did not like to see a mission run its work in a beggarly way. That shows the spirit of the time.

In view of such a situation, the position of the infant Church can be easily imagined ; it hangs on to the mission like the tail of an elephant. Happily many Christian leaders have realised this top-heavy situation, and are working and praying for a speedy change. The Church, not the mission, is the permanent organisation in this as well as in other lands.

It is reported that the total number of communicant Christians in China at the present time amounts to 360,000. Out of that number there are no less than 24,000 men and women who are salaried workers of the missions and churches, engaged in evangelistic, educational, medical, and other forms of service. In other words, one in every fifteen church members is in the employ of the Missions. Most of these workers are inadequately trained and poorly supported. They hold in the nature of things, the position of " native helpers " to the missionary leaders. It could not have been otherwise. Speaking broadly, the missionary has had the opportunity for getting a better education, he has more experience, a wider knowledge in mission and Church affairs, and greater Christian background. The Chinese helper has had very few of these advantages. He has therefore to be contented to hold a secondary position in the mission churches. The missionary has the say in the policy of the work and the disbursement of funds. Sometimes he chooses to seek the advice of his Chinese workers ; often he does not.

Now let this question be asked : Who is after all the helper, the Chinese worker or the missionary ? The young Christian Church would make bold to say positively : In the truest sense of the word the missionary is the helper to the Christian Church in China, a position which is his crowning glory in the Church. Two or three missionaries are now acting in one of the independent Chinese Christian churches in North China as deacons and other similar church officers. Such a practice is, we believe, sound in principle. It is only human, however, when the time comes for a real change, for devolution, or transfer of control, we find some who are not ready to make the sacrifice—for it is a real sacrifice for those who have held the reins of things for so long to be willing to give them over to others. The excuse generally given is that " the time is not yet ripe for such a radical change," and " the Church is unable to assume such a responsibility."

While Christianity is an oriental religion, it has come to China by way of Europe and America. It did not come in its primitive simplicity, but with many accretions acquired during its spread in western lands. There are no less than 140 autonomous missionary Societies working in various parts of China at the present time. While in general the purpose of all these various bodies is one and the same, viz., the preaching of Christ to the people of this land who are still in spiritual darkness, yet each society or missionary organisation has its own special interests, features, temperaments, and points of emphasis. This in itself is bewildering to the Chinese, both within and without the Church, especially when denominational differences are being emphasised to the extent that the members of one society or church are incapable of working in unity and harmony with those of another. A missionary teacher once said that his work in China was to give to the Chinese correct definitions regarding the particular teaching of his Church. One wonders whether that was really his main task in China.

Out of the 1,713 counties in China, with the exception of only 126, every one has a mission place in it. The whole of China except the special areas (Mongolia, Sinkiang, etc.) is being claimed by one or more missionary societies as a " sphere of influence " in a religious sense of the phrase. When a field is " claimed " it does not necessarily mean that the field is really occupied, and the work of evangelisation thoroughly done—not by any means. Different types of teaching, different forms of church government, different lines of emphasis, different types of activity are evident in the areas claimed by different missions. It results that the conception of Christianity held by Chinese Christians varies widely in different sections.

Without any clear understanding of the causes which give rise to the many different denominations of the West, it is only natural that the Chinese followers of the Master should find themselves unable to come into very deep appreciation of Western denominationalism. These differences do not seem to us so vital to the life of the Christian Church as they do to our friends from the West. Chinese Christians welcome union in every possible way, and are only held back from much closer union by the inability of their missionary friends to go with them. Happily in recent years the desire for closer co-operation is growing among missionaries, and some progress along this line has already been made. Union institutions for higher education have been established, amalgamations of organisations doing similar work and organic union of churches of the same and of different denominations have taken place, frequent union meetings and conferences have been held, and in a number of other ways the Christian forces in China are trying to " dwell together in unity." For this we are profoundly thankful to the Lord.

In considering the problems between the missions and the churches, and between the missionaries and the Chinese Christians, we are not blind to the wonderful work done by the missions for the benefit of the Church, nor of the noble example given us by a large number of our missionary co-workers. The Christian Church in China owes its origin to the work of the missions. We shall always appreciate

the great work done for China by the missions and
their missionaries. Nevertheless we have boldly
stated some of the problems affecting the relationship between the missions and the churches in the
hope that in the days to come the work will be more
efficient and mutually helpful than in the past.
For, after all, whether we speak of missions or
churches, men of the West or of the East, the chief
end in view is absolutely the same.

There is another group of problems which is
more closely related to the Church itself. Let us
make mention of a few of them.

The word of our Lord, " The poor have the
gospel preached to them " has its fulfilment in
China. Until quite recently most of those who have
accepted the Christian faith have been men and
women of the humbler and less influential classes.
The better educated and more influential people
of the land generally looked upon Christianity with
distrust and contempt. It was, in their estimation,
a religion for the unlearned and ignorant. It was
quite beneath their dignity to take any serious
notice of this foreign religion. The Bible was too
simple for them and the church too common a place.
This was true in the past, it is also true to a large
extent at the present time, though a considerable
change has taken place. It is estimated that
thirty-five per cent. of the men, and sixty-five per
cent. of the women in the Christian Church in

China to-day are still unable to read or write. That means they have no direct access to the Word of God. Because of lack of education, the Bible is not an open book to these brethren in Christ. What a drawback! They are thus deprived of one of the most important means for the development of the Christian life. This is indeed lamentable. It constitutes a pressing problem not merely of the Church, but of the nation as well. Illiteracy is, no doubt, one of the greatest hindrances in the way of the progress of the Christian faith in China.

Realising the danger of ignorance many servants of God are doing their utmost to fight against this common enemy of the Church. There is a movement on foot to secure in the shortest possible time a Bible-reading Church. Various means are being used to gain the desired end. Among other methods the use of the national phonetic script is being pushed with great zeal and determination. Adult illiterates have been taught to read the Bible in a very short time. Portions of the Scriptures, the whole of the New Testament, and other literature, are being widely circulated and used. The work of the Phonetic Promotion Committee of the China Continuation Committee, headed by Miss S. J. Garland, of the China Inland Mission, is doing very effective work. The motto of the committee is "Every Christian a Bible reader, and every Christian a teacher of illiterates." We are glad to say that in this phonetic propaganda the Chinese Government and a number of the larger Chinese publishing houses are also taking a lively interest. When the enemy of illiteracy is conquered, the Church as well as the government will have done a great deal

Modern missions have made the question of the Church's independence of the Mission a burning problem. No healthy Christian can be satisfied in remaining in a position of dependence. Every Chinese Christian says "amen" to the strong words of our Japanese friend, the Rev. Masahisa Uemura, when he voiced the keen desire of his fellow Christians in Japan by saying that "To depend upon the pocket of foreigners for money to pay the bills is not a situation which ought to satisfy the moral sense of Japanese Christians. Likewise in the realm of religious thought, is it not shameful to accept opinions ready-made, relying on the experience of others instead of one's own ? Those of us who are insisting on the independence of the Church in our country are not moved by narrow nationalistic ideas. . . . We are moved by the positive power of a great ideal. Every nation has its special character-istics. . . . Is it not a great duty we owe to God and to mankind, to develop the religious talent of our people, and to contribute our share to the religious ideas of the world ? " We believe the Church in the country of the Rising Sun has made much progress because of this spirit of independence.

Such a spirit of independence is, in a measure, in existence in the Chinese Church also. It has manifested itself in directions both healthy and otherwise, and thus creates a real problem of the Church. Some, dissatisfied with the foreign dominance now existing in the church, are finding it difficult to get along with the missionary, and have as a result of much wounded friendship established independent Churches which are beyond the control of the missionary. When independence is the result of such causes it is indeed regrettable. A house built on such sandy foundation cannot possibly weather the storm for long. But this is fortunately only one of the motives leading to a desire for an independent Chinese Church. There exist to-day in China independent churches built on the solid foundation of faith in Christ and maintaining a most cordial relationship with the missionaries from whose hands they have received the Gospel of Christ. In some of these churches the missionary is performing a true ministry of help to his Chinese fellow Christians. His word of advice is freely given and readily taken, and the relationship is all that could be desired. While the Church in China must move along independent lines, its ideal is not independence so much as co-operation. The latter is a much larger word than the former. This is true not only in the Church but in the international relationships of the nations as well.

In connection with the whole subject of developing self-reliance in the Church there are the three ideals that have long been in the minds of all who are seeking for the growth of the Church life in China, namely : self-support, self-government, and self-propagation. A healthy Church requires all these elements of development. Situated as the Church is at the present time in China, many problems are involved in bringing about a state of things where those conditions apply, and they need very careful and prayerful consideration.

Speaking as a whole no noteworthy progress in the matter of self-support has been made in the mission churches in China. The attitude and practice of the missions in developing self-support vary greatly. Some urge the immediate realisation of entire financial support by each church from the time of its organisation ; some believe it is a matter of growth to be attained by degrees ; some measure the amount of control to be given to the Church by the amount of financial support given by its members. If the Chinese people are generous supporters of non-Christian religions, and are willing givers to all kinds of benevolent work, as we no doubt believe they are, then the slow progress in attaining self-support by the Christian Churches should certainly cause us to pause and ask ourselves what is the root cause of this stagnation.

In our opinion the matter is largely a question of Training. It is not an uncommon thing for the Chinese believers to think that the mission has unlimited wealth, and that there is no real necessity for the few cash the members of the Church are in a position to give. What is the good of adding one drop of water to the ocean, people ask. Therefore it is of great importance to Christians to feel that the giving for the support of the Christian cause, however small, is a means of grace and a great privilege, and is not merely a duty to be performed. Furthermore, the giving of money to the Church does not exhaust the whole question of self-support. The giving of time, thought, labour, prayer, and love, are equally acceptable in the sight of the Unseen, if not more so. The relationship of the mission and the Church should never be a dollar-and-cent one.

Perhaps it will prove interesting to note the progress that has been made along this particular line in some of the churches which are entirely independent of the missions. In a recent Conference of the Chinese Christian churches in North China it was found that there are nine or ten such churches in the provinces of Shantung and Chihli. The total income of these bodies for the year 1920-1921 amounted to $23,000 silver. This amount included some money for building purposes. The total membership of these churches is 2,600. Knowing the former condition of these small groups of believers one is gratified for the advance made thus far.

If the question of self-government is looked upon, either by the missionary or by the Chinese Christian, as an attempt to get more power on the one hand, or to withhold it on the other—a state of things common in the political dealings of the nations—we may as well abandon the struggle, because we think that such a motive is wrong. The matter must be approached from the point of view of helping the young Church to begin to shoulder its own responsibilities. Political methods and scheming for power are unworthy of the object to be attained. It is no doubt true that with many churches the time has not yet come to assume full control and full self-government; but we do believe the time has come for starting a movement in that direction. No buying-and-selling method is capable of dealing with this essentially spiritual problem.

There is more evidence in the Chinese Church in recent years that a spirit of self-propagation is developing. Many signs of life and strength are revealed here, but we shall limit ourselves to only two incidents.

The name of General Feng Yu-hsiang, Governor of the Province of Shensi, stands out as a notable example among individual Christians who have exerted a positive Christian influence. Since he became a follower of Christ the greater part of the

10,000 men under his command have been won to the Christian faith. Wherever he and his men have been they have left behind them a people full of appreciation and gratitude. This means all the more because the general feeling of the people is strongly opposed to the military classes.

In team work the movement of the Chinese Home Missionary Society is worthy of special mention. Thousands of Chinese Christians are taking a deep interest in this missionary enterprise. The distant province of Yunnan has been selected as its mission field. Recently the home missionary society of the Presbyterian churches in the Manchurian provinces has been linked up with the Chinese Home Missionary Society. This movement was started by a small group of Christian ladies at Kuling three years ago, after very earnest prayer and waiting upon God. Ever since it was launched it has been making fine progress. Nine Chinese missionaries are now working in the province of Yunnan in the south-west of China, and two ordained pastors are labouring in the province of Hei Lung Chiang, in the North. Chinese Christians of many churches in almost all the provinces in China, as well as Chinese abroad, have joined in the support of this movement. When a Church is on fire with zeal for the spreading of the message of salvation, we know for certain it has life ; it has in

Another problem that is confronting the young Church in the East is its relation to matters of a national or international character. In the recent patriotic movement led by the student classes of this country, the Christians have shown their sympathy, and, in not a few cases, given their support. We believe the Church should be the director of the public conscience, and should be the leader in every activity that works for enlightenment, righteousness and truth. The Church as an organisation should, however, not be mixed with matters of a political nature. Political parties are not blind to the fact that if the churches can be induced to serve their political purposes the advantage to them will not be small; but the Church should stand firm and remain a purely religious and spiritual institution.

The whole world knows of the strained relationship between China and her nearest neighbour, Japan. The Chinese Christian feels as keenly as the rest of his fellow countrymen the injustice of the high-handed treatment of China by the military masters of that country. There is, however, no ill feeling against the Japanese people on the part of the Chinese Christians and of all intelligent people in China. But we feel it is the duty of every lover of truth and justice to hate injustice and despotism and fight for righteousness and freedom. Has Christianity a helping hand to extend to save the situation ? Have the Christians of these two nations anything to say or do ? Can those who would live and die for the same Christian principles stand together against the common foe, irrespective of nationality ? Are we willing and daring enough to stand for right against might ? The world has yet to see what the forces of the Christian army can do, in the strength of their Lord, in helping to solve such world problems of which there are many.

The intellectual awakening in China, commonly known as the Renaissance Movement, presents to the Christian Church a wonderful opportunity as well as a real problem. The attitude of the more educated and influential classes towards the Christian religion and its followers has greatly changed in recent years. The purpose of the Church in seeking the good of China is generally recognised. During the recent famine in North China a large part of the more than seventeen million silver dollars raised for famine relief was entrusted to the Christian leaders for distribution among the suffering people. Missionaries have been appealed to by both officials of the government and those opposed to it for settling disputes between them. Many are willing to study the teaching of Christ, and some have openly accepted the faith, and joined the Church. One of the oldest, if not the oldest non-Christian daily paper, which has the largest circulation in the whole of China, was willing to issue a special Christmas number last year, which contained many especially written articles on the significance of the advent of Christ, and the various activities of the Christian movement in China. The country has an open door and the people have an open heart for the Gospel message.

In this connection there is also another line of development. The New Thought Movement has helped the educated youth of China to think for themselves. They want to ask " Why ? " about everything, and to take nothing for granted. Naturally they apply the same principle to Christianity. They study the history and the teaching of the Christian Church in that critical attitude. Some say that Christianity has served its day and is no use to the scientific world of to-day ; some declare that æsthetics can take the place of religion ; others are positive that Christianity has done more harm than good in the world ; still others think the Christian religion is nothing but foolishness and superstition and has no place in the present enlightened age. More has been written against the Christian faith, its teaching, its organisation and its followers, in the last two or three years than perhaps in all the past years combined.

All this opens up a remarkable opportunity for the Church to bear witness for its Lord and Master. But one asks : " Is the Church ready to meet this unusual situation ? " " Where is the prophet of the Lord that hears the Message so much needed at the present hour ? " " Where is the timely Christian literature that will really meet the needs of the people who are seeking for light and truth ? " " Where are the leaders ? " " Are the various Christian forces sufficiently awakened to the significance of the present situation ? " " Are they in thought and action sufficiently united to capture the opportunity and make a great advance ? " Think of the results of success, or the consequences of failure, to the Church as well as to the nation !

Leaders of the Church are looking with eager expectation toward the National Christian Conference to be held in Shanghai early in May, 1922. For the first time in the history of the Church in China a Conference is to be held composed of approximately 1,000 Church and Mission delegates, half Chinese and half missionaries, elected by their respective Church and Mission authorities. The theme of the Conference is " The Chinese Church." The preparation of material for presentation to the Conference has been entrusted to five Commissions. These Commissions will deal with " The Present State of Christianity in China "; " The Future Task of the Church "; " The Message of the Church "; " The Development of Leadership in the Work of the Church "; and " Co-operation and Co-ordination in the Work of the Church." We hope that some of the problems we have indicated in this paper will find expression and solution at this great Christian gathering of next year. We hope the Conference will mark another milestone of Christian progress in this ancient land of ours. We confidently expect that henceforth the Chinese Church will more and more realise its true place and will speedily take up its burdens and responsibilities to the glory of Almighty God.

In the limited space at our disposal we have endeavoured to state some of the more pressing problems of the Church in China at the present time. Each one of these problems would require special treatment to call attention to all the facts which enter into a solution and to discuss them in relation to the problem, but that is not possible at the present time. If this paper in any measure arouses a keener interest in the work of the Christian movement in China, we shall be happy.

Let us remind ourselves that after all the supreme problem of the Church and of its members is a spiritual one. It is along these lines we believe that one must seek the real solution of all the problems that are confronting the infant Church of the Far East. Let us, therefore, earnestly and definitely pray for THE OUTPOURING OF A DOUBLE PORTION OF THE SPIRIT OF GOD UPON BOTH THE MISSIONS AND CHURCHES THAT ARE WORKING IN THIS ANCIENT LAND OF CATHAY.

January, 1922,
Shanghai.